RICARDO
LEGORRETA
ARCHITECTS

Ricardo Legorreta

Víctor Legorreta

Noé Castro

RICARDO LEGORRETA
ARCHITECTS

Edited, with Introduction by John V. Mutlow

Principal photography by Lourdes Legorreta

RIZZOLI
NEW YORK

Library of Congress Cataloging-in-Publication Data

Ricardo Legorreta, architects / edited with introduction by John
        V. Mutlow ; preface by Ricardo Legorreta.
            p.   cm.
        Includes bibliographical references.
        ISBN 0–8478–2023–8 (hc)
            1. Legorreta Vilchis, Ricardo—Criticism and interpretation.
        2. Architecture, Modern—20th century—Mexico.
        3. Architecture, Modern—20th century—West (U.S.)
        I. Mutlow, John V.
        NA759.L44R53   1997   96–47059
        720′ .92—DC21   CIP

Designed by Marcus Ratliff, Inc., New York

Front jacket photograph: Pershing Square, Los Angeles, California, 1994
Back jacket photograph: Greenberg House, Los Angeles, California, 1991
Title spread: Greenberg House, Los Angeles, California, 1991
Opposite: Rancho Santa Fe House, Rancho Sante Fe, California, 1987
Frontispiece: Monterrey Central Library, Monterrey, Mexico, 1994

Printed and bound in Italy

CONTENTS

PREFACE

Mexico is a country of architects. We Mexicans are builders; we are all architects. I am not an exception. Although I do not come from an artistic family, I have always lived surrounded by architecture; I spent my childhood visiting villages, haciendas, convents, and churches. This world of Mexican spaces filled my life in such a natural way that light, walls, color, mystery, and water, with all their beauty, became part of me. I am not an exception. That is the way we Mexicans are.

I don't remember when I decided to become an architect; it just happened, and when I communicated it to my parents I received their total support.

The romanticism, beauty, richness, light, and color of Mexico—but above all, its people—have become an obsession for me.

My father taught me spirituality, social conscience, and a deep love for Mexico; and José Villagrán, the love for architecture. From Luis Barragán, Chucho Reyes, and Pedro Coronel, I learned about color and beauty.

These influences, together with my passion and romanticism, have become the pillars of my professional life.

The contrasting realities, humanism, and magic of Mexico helped me realize that architecture must be human and at the service of society and people.

Mexican wall
You are
Support for roofs
Limit of property and dreams
Source of inspiration
Witness to our loves
Mexican wall
Essence of our architecture....
When in certain moments
In our history
Mexico has been invaded

By a foreign culture
The wall hides
And seems to disappear
But suddenly
Together with the people
Comes back screaming
Recovering its presence.
The Mexican wall
Will never die
If it ever happened
Mexico would die with it.

Beautiful space
Human serene and luminous
Full of color and mystery
Magnificent space...
You are architecture.

Mexican villages with their vernacular architecture are an example of the correct Mexican lifestyle, successfully mixing ethnic, cultural, and economic differences in a human and harmonious environment. They have been and will remain endless sources of inspiration and happiness.

Surrounded by this magical world, I have devoted my life to the most beautiful profession, knowing that the road is not long but endless, and that when we disappear, if our ideals are worthy somebody will pick up our flag and continue.

We live in a period of speed: in order to manage it we need to work together, looking at technology as a tool not as a goal, keeping the basic values of humanism, avoiding superficiality, solving people's needs without serving power and materialism.

I have worked with my partners, Noé Castro, to whom I am deeply grateful for friendship, advice, and support, and my son Víctor, who together with a young, enthusiastic, and talented team has brought a promising future, assuring improvement and the continuation of our efforts as well as the immense happiness of family collaboration.

My gratitude to my daughter Lourdes for the talent, sensibility, and love that produced most of the photographs in this book.

At this time of my life, my meditations touch the deepest parts of my soul and mind.

Ricardo Legorreta
Mexico City, September 1996

Earth and sky
Light and color
Walls and plaster
Essence of beauty
Spirituality and life
They produce happiness.

If architecture
Doesn't contribute
To human peace and happiness
It deserves to disappear.

Happiness
Is in finding worthwhile goals
That contribute
To human well-being
Happiness
Is not in achievements
But in effort.
Happiness
Is giving
Not receiving.

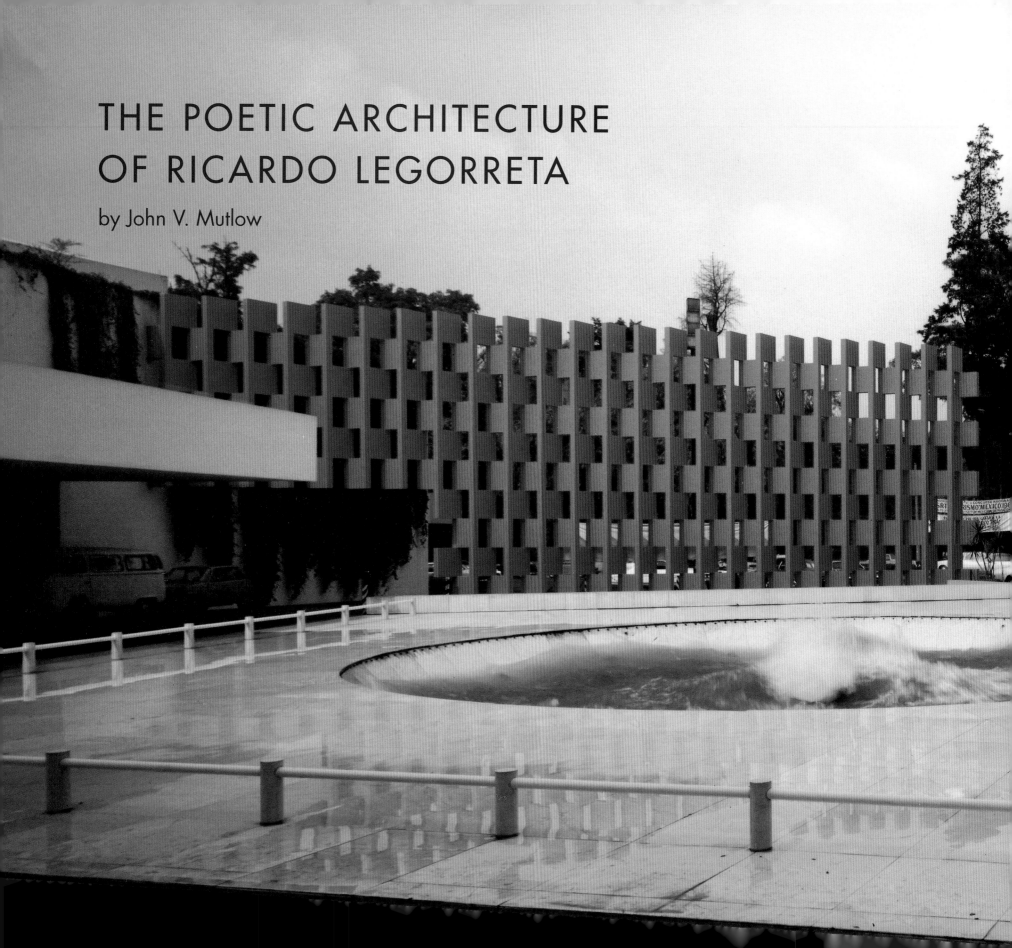

THE POETIC ARCHITECTURE
OF RICARDO LEGORRETA

by John V. Mutlow

On arriving in Mexico City on New Year's Eve in 1968, I became immersed in the architecture of Ricardo Legorreta. By chance, I was booked into the recently completed Camino Real Mexico Hotel, an extraordinary design by Legorreta that was to become the world's introduction to his work. Entering the hotel after experiencing the hustle and bustle of the airport and the intensity of the city's traffic, I knew that I had come to a special place. The only entrance from the street was through a serrated, shocking pink—actually magenta—screen, a void in the massive white walls that led into a motor court surrounding a low fountain with undulating waves that emanated peace, quiet, and solitude. From there, under a canopied drop-off, one entered the spacious lobby, where one could look back in turn to the motor court and entry screen.

Once inside the calm, minimalist lobby, I was greeted by a beautiful mural by Rufino Tamayo on the facing wall. Another mural, in gold, by Mathias Goeritz, at the top of a grand staircase leading to the conference center, seemed to suggest the presence of sun inside the building. At one side of the lobby a bar overlooked a tranquil, azure reflecting pool.

Throughout the lobby and public areas of the hotel, each space is articulated at right angles to the one preceding it, so the viewer takes in a space entirely before entering the next one. Direct axial, formalist approaches are avoided, so one's perception and awareness of the space become the basis for exploration. Legorreta's intention was to create a true sense of spaciousness in which one's attention is focused on a piece of art, an intimate corner, or the guests themselves, rather than on simply moving through the space. This relaxed and gracious introduction to the modern architecture of Mexico was also my first encounter with Ricardo Legorreta's architecture.

Prior to designing the hotel, in 1964 Legorreta had completed the Chrysler Factory in Toluca, Mexico, his office's first major work. It embodied a blend of the spatial qualities of Mexican vernacular architecture with the more rigid and rationalist forms typical of José Villagrán, whose office Legorreta joined after graduating from the Universidad Nacional Autónoma de México. Villagrán was in the forefront of the modern rationalist movement in Mexico of the 1960s, and it was in his office that Legorreta learned the craft of building, the myriad details necessary to realize architecture. But Legorreta did not support an architectural movement based primarily on rationalism; he felt that such an architecture did not represent the Mexican lifestyle, which he sees as characterized by an enjoyment of life, by changing direction at a moment's notice, and by an afternoon siesta.

At the Chrysler Factory, a grand colonnade of trees lines one edge of the entrance plaza, which focuses dramatically on two conical towers that have become the symbol for the plant, but which in reality function as water cisterns and an auditorium. At the dedication of the factory, Legorreta was introduced to Luis Barragán by the artist Mathias Goeritz, with whom Legorreta had collaborated on the conical towers. Legorreta asked Barragán to comment on the building and received the following response: "You need to pay more attention to the landscaping; it is an integral part of architecture." Legorreta, clearly, has never forgotten this encounter with Barragán.

Previous pages: Motor court, Camino Real Mexico Hotel, Mexico City, 1968

Opposite: Chrysler Factory, Toluca, Mexico, 1964

LANDSCAPING AND THE INFLUENCE OF LUIS BARRAGÁN

The meeting with Barragán proved providential for Legorreta, but not in the way most critics have thought, that is, not in Legorreta's treatment of the wall and use of color, but in the integration of landscape as an essential element of architecture.

In the late 1960s, Barragán collaborated with Legorreta on the landscaping of the Camino Real Mexico Hotel, where a large courtyard is a center for social activities and smaller patios lend privacy and identity to clusters of guest rooms. Such a lush enclave and smaller refuges recall the various enclosed outdoor and indoor/outdoor spaces that characterize Hispanic and pre-Columbian architecture and which remain important sources for Mexican architecture today.

In the Hispanic tradition, water is typically incorporated in courtyards and patios, and Legorreta displays water prominently in the forecourt at the Camino Real hotel. In the patio at the Renault Factory in Gómez Palacio, Mexico, of 1985, and in the quiet water channels at Solana in Dallas, Texas, of 1991, water is used in a relatively traditional way. But water can also be used in unconventional ways, as Legorreta demonstrates so enthusiastically with the exuberant ensemble of fountains, cascades, water stairs, and terraced pools at the Camino Real Ixtapa Hotel of 1981, an extraordinary collection of spaces for the guests' enjoyment.

For the Solana mixed-use development, water, walls, and a tower landmark identify the complex from the highway. At the Monterrey Central Library in Mexico, of 1994, the building and an adjacent lake are joined by a grand staircase that cascades into the water, as if a fishing line were being cast into the lake.

Legorreta's signature integration of landscape, walls, and building is most fully realized, however, at the Renault Factory, where the river-washed stone of the wall plane is linked so well to the harsh environment of the high desert. Here, Legorreta paid homage to

Children's Discovery Museum,
San Jose, California, 1989

the desert: the stones both soften the edge of the flat, stark terrain and connect it naturally to the building. In another instance, the House in Sonoma, California, of 1993, is linked to a vast open space of rolling hills by grid after grid of new landscaping. For the house in Rancho Santa Fe, California, of 1987, terraced stone stairs adorned with sculptural spheres and clay pots respond to the wall planes to create a wonderfully unified ambience. And, at the Greenberg House in Los Angeles, of 1991, the masterful asymmetrical composition of palm trees, cactus, gravel lawn, and house demonstrates the extraordinary power that landscape and architecture can bring to each other when they become one. Such accomplishments become even more noteworthy considering that there is no separate profession of landscape architecture in Mexico.

MINIMALISM AND THE ELEMENTS OF ARCHITECTURE

Legorreta's use of the wall plane, light, scale, geometry, emotion, and color has received the most extensive attention, and when assembled in his particular way these elements constitute what has often been referred to as the Legorreta Style.

Wall

In Mexico, it is the wall itself that dominates, not the floor or roof planes combined with it to form architectural space. Walls are used in more powerful ways in Mexico than in other places, to suggest strength, tragedy, peace, or light. Here, establishing property ownership via a wall is more important than projecting the image of the house as icon. Walls are the vehicle through which the great Mexican muralists such as David Alfaro Siqueiros, José Clemente Orozco, and Diego Rivera depicted the most potent human emotions—joy, pain, or the struggle for freedom. It was completely natural, then, that the wall became Legorreta's most important architectural element. At the Renault Factory, the wall actually becomes the building; it hovers, long and low, behind the dunes, evoking the loneliness and emptiness of the desert.

Invited to participate in the design of the master plan for Solana, Legorreta was responsible for establishing architectural character for a business complex newly created on barren prairie land. Legorreta asked the members of the design team to visit an old convent with him so they could understand his perception of walls and their meaning. There, walls enclose individual compounds and provide an overall unity to the entire complex, yet they respect the unique architectural character of each compound.

Renault Factory, Gómez Palacio,
Durango, Mexico, 1985

For his first project outside Mexico—the Montalbán House in Hollywood, of 1985—Legorreta used a similar approach. There, high in the hills, the back of the house opens to panoramic views of Los Angeles. The front, however, presents to the street a composition of earth-tone volumes enclosed by solid walls that define various parts of the house but do not reveal their use.

Light

Mexico's mountainous terrain, high altitudes, and lush vegetation favor an unusual quality of natural light that Mexican architects have traditionally used to

their advantage. The everchanging rays of the sun glare at midday to wash out bright colors and reduce them to pastel shades. In the late afternoon and in the rainy season, however, the reverse happens: colors absorb the yellow and red rays of the sun or moisture from rain and become almost iridescent.

Legorreta well understands the importance of the changing quality of light. For him, light gives life and character to architectural space, and he uses it very consciously to manipulate the effect of planes, materials, and textures. The screens in the Camino Real Mexico Hotel, for instance, reflect and diffuse rays of light dramatically into space. Vertical columnar "screens" at the City of the Arts, in Mexico City, of 1994, are designed specifically to cast rays of light in patterns across the floor. Often in his architecture, windows are not strictly windows but voids in a plane that articulate light to enhance a space in a particular way. Barrel vaults bounce light in multiple directions, and water not only adds depth to space but also reflects shimmering light on surfaces.

Scale

The scale of a building or space is determined by the relationship between a building or space and its parts, and is thus an element that indicates whether a form or space is perceived as intimate, monumental, or in between. To achieve the small-scale intimacy of his own Mexico City office, of 1966, Legorreta used a restricted palette of materials and designed furniture to blend in with the warren of small rooms and circulation elements that descend the steep hillside. Conversely, at the Camino Real Ixtapa Hotel, he expressed monumentalism by articulating the building "as" the mountain, with guest rooms cascading down to the beach and ocean. The vast scale is countered, however, in the guest rooms, where minimal materials, simple furniture, individual private terraces, and special color provide a sense of intimacy.

Geometry

In the larger, more important buildings, where monumentality is desirable, geometry becomes a crucial element of Legorreta's architectural vocabulary. At the Monterrey Central Library, in northern Mexico, of 1994, a cube is embedded in a cylinder that terminates with two descending triangles. At the San Antonio Main Library, in Texas, of 1995, the dominant geometry is two rotated cubes; while in the administration tower at the City of the Arts, a cylinder houses research offices and a triangular prism accommodates circulation. Barrel vaults are used to articulate or identify a notable space, as in the library at the Central Building of the City of the Arts or the public foyer at Solana. Vernacular forms are also an integral part of Legorreta's vocabulary, particularly the dome, which he incorporates in the roofs of the School of the Visual Arts and of the Metropolitan Cathedral in Managua, Nicaragua, of 1993.

Emotion

Legorreta understands Mexican culture as one infused with emotion, mystery, and exuberance. To create an architecture that responds to such qualities, Legorreta layers his buildings and landscapes with emotive space and forms. He believes that users must become emotionally involved with space; they must react to it or become engaged with it. This attitude is opposite to that of strict modernism, which attempts to disengage the user by providing universal, anonymous space.

The emotional aspect of Legorreta's architecture is most apparent in his public projects, where spaces and forms are carefully orchestrated with light and shadow for dramatic effect. He also brings to his work a sense of humor and playfulness: the oversized, vibrantly colored, sculptural pears at the Camino Real Mexico Hotel, the large watermelon slices at the Camino Real Ixtapa Hotel, or the less obvious purple cylinders on the terrace of the San Antonio Main Library reflect this spirit.

Chula Vista Library, Chula Vista, California, 1995

Color

Most references to Legorreta's work stress color as the primary force, but this is an incorrect premise. For Legorreta, color is an integral part of the world around us, a symbol of our emotions, a fundamental, vernacular element. He uses it to enrich space, to dramatize or evoke an emotional response, or to enhance one's experience. And even though color may sometimes become more important than the surface on which it is painted, as evidenced by the pigeon rookery at Solana or the bell tower at Pershing Square in Los Angeles, of 1994, it is never the impetus of the work or the primary force behind it, but simply a perfectly natural part of it.

Legorreta understands color as a crucial aspect of life in Mexico; it is something that stems naturally from deep cultural roots. Color is an integral part of the Mexican vernacular and can be seen everywhere, from the hillside town of Guanajuato with its wonderful display of rich and varied hues on the houses cascading down the mountainside, to paintings such as those of Pedro Coronel with their completely free use of color. At the Camino Real Mexico Hotel, fuschia screens tint the light as it is reflected into the lobby and hallways. Blue barrel vaults at Solana both intensify the light's impact and bounce it throughout the spaces. The massive yellow walls of the Renault Factory, and the purple bars and freestanding column screen at the City of the Arts, charge spaces with energy and reinforce their presence.

Legorreta's use of color has been more restrained in the United States, where he has recently received several important commissions, especially in California and Texas. This tendency can be seen in the Greenberg, Montalbán, and Rancho Santa Fe houses in California, and even in large, public mixed-use projects such as Solana. This more restrained use of color is partially due to the more conservative nature of the clients, but more importantly, it demonstrates the point that color is a vernacular, cultural element, and therefore specific to its location.

A HUMANE POSITION

Although Legorreta's clients are mostly affluent, this has not altered the architect's social conscience and his belief that one of the first responsibilities of the architect is to the people who will use his buildings. At the IBM Technical Center in Mexico City, of 1977, concern for the well-being of the worker was an important part of the design. There, managers and workers occupy the same spaces. Assembly lines were designed like desks in offices, and open spaces and courtyards were carefully worked into the overall plan to extend the social spaces.

At El Rosario, a public housing project in Mexico City, of 1976, Legorreta carefully designed the plans for the individual apartments to make the best use of their limited space. To humanize the monolithic residential blocks, walled-in drying terraces were designed to project beyond the building facade to provide rhythm and break down its scale, and places were created for people to just sit, watch, or play.

Legorreta's architecture derives from his interpretation of the Mexican vernacular with its freedom from rules, enviable simplicity, and embrace of mystery. This is then transformed into his own particular spirit of modernism, one in which space is articulated through layered planes, where a limited range of materials is used, details are minimal, light and color are introduced to intensify an effect, and landscape is carefully integrated with the built project. While this approach often produces an architecture of considerable beauty, more important for Legorreta is that it is an architecture created with poetry, one that can touch the heart and, most of all, one that is from the heart.

IBM Factory, Guadalajara, Jalisco, Mexico, 1975

INTERVIEW WITH RICARDO LEGORRETA

This interview between John V. Mutlow and Ricardo Legorreta took place at the Legorreta Arquitectos office in Mexico City on May 28, 1996.

JM: I would like initially to discuss personal activities or events that have influenced your life and affected your architecture.

RL: I would say there were two events or experiences. One was a serious illness. The true feeling of dying changed my view of life by making me realize that health, friendship, and human concerns are the most important values. The second was my struggle to understand Mexico's real personality, the truth about Mexico. My viewpoint has changed: when I was young I looked at objects and buildings as pure aesthetics, but little by little I have discovered that there is more depth to them. As an example, you might say initially that the vernacular architecture of Mexico is very beautiful, but then you find that there is depth behind the beauty. I realized this the moment we started to work outside Mexico. When you travel or work in another culture, you realize that many aspects of life that you take for granted are very valuable. My experience working in the United States has substantially changed how I view my roots; in fact, I am now more appreciative of them.

JM: In discussing your roots, we began examining precolonial and pre-Columbian architecture. Can you identify specific references or influences that have had a strong effect on your architecture?

RL: Regarding light, one place that has had a strong influence on me is Monte Albán in Oaxaca. I will always remember this place. There is a specific hour when I love to go there, during sunset, when mystery, elegance, and spirituality are present.

With pre-Columbian architecture we have to meditate on simplicity because it is based on simple masses, but at the same time it can accept very complicated elements, such as the carvings in the stone.

Another influence is my experiences traveling alone to the villages of Mexico. I have taken about four or five trips by myself in my Jeep. Being alone is a completely different experience. You are not sharing any comments, thoughts, or ideas with anyone else; you can draw a direct connection with the local people. One time, for example, I was traveling in my Jeep with a basket of wine, cheese, and bread. I stopped at an old hacienda to look and to study it. Suddenly a farmer came out with his maize, and I started talking to him. I offered him a tequila, and we ended up conversing for two hours. When I was leaving, after several tequilas, he said to me, "Take care, lock your car." That is when I realized that this man was supposed to hate me. He was a very poor man, and there I was with my brand new Jeep, cheese, and wine.

Through such experiences, I realized the responsibility of working as an architect. It is very easy yet very difficult to be an architect in Mexico, because you are designing projects with large financial investments, and at the same time your roots lie in—and fellow citizens live in—conditions that are economically poor but still spiritually rich. This realization has led me to devote my efforts to designing architecture that truly serves people and makes them happy.

JM: Could you discuss an example where you have integrated this sense of social consciousness into your work?

RL: One good example was the IBM Factory in Guadalajara. The worker became the most important element in designing the factory. I recommended that we break away from IBM's white-and-blue trademark colors and design for the workers in a human sense. The client listened to me and supported the idea. We put the assembly lines right next to the offices, and designed the assembly lines as if we were designing desks. The plan permits the open spaces to be used by the workers for family parties or gatherings, on weekends, or after work.

A second example was the El Papalote Children's Museum in Mexico City. In a sense, I didn't pay attention to the adults' comments about what a children's museum should be. I intended to design for the children and provide them with a sense of freedom and imagination. That's why adults, after an hour in the museum, become nervous—they are in a child's world. Social responsibility exists not only in low-cost housing; I see it at all levels, and not just in the sense of humanitarian deeds for poor people.

JM: In Mexico you have a wonderful, rich history—the pre-Columbian and colonial. The culture in which you live today is also rich, a mix of the vernacular and the modern. What references to vernacular or to the Modern Movement have you used in your architecture?

RL: The vernacular transcends the rigidity that architects learn in school, in which there always has to be a reason for doing everything. In vernacular there is no reason, just pure emotion. Why do certain windows have certain dimensions? Just because the people like it. One day when I was driving, I stopped at a house—actually, it was just a room. It was beautifully painted blue and yellow. . . . It was great! As I started to take photographs, the owner came out. I said, "Your house is marvelous! How did you choose your colors? Why did you paint it like that?" He looked at me in a strange way and said, "I just like it." So I have learned about placing elements where I feel they should be, without any explanation.

JM: This ties directly into your approach to architecture. What is it in general?

RL: I think that a space, or a building, has to have an emotional reason to exist. I call this a philosophy. It has to mean something. It is not only about saying, "This room is going to be very beautiful"; it is that the room, house, or building has to have a philosophy, like the IBM Factory, a real social mixture. But my main approach is, "What do I want to do with this project?" You have to let the idea of the project digest or evolve inside you before you start to design. I never design first. For example, this weekend I went to Napa Valley [California] to see a site for a new house. Right now I have an insight—I don't know what it is exactly, but I am starting to think about how I will approach the challenge of building on the site and for a specific client.

JM: People who visit and study your architecture clearly see a series of elements, such as your particular use of light, planes, proportion, and color, that could be described as your signature. How important are these elements in your architecture, and at what point do you introduce them into the design process?

RL: They are tools more than they are the final objectives of my architecture, and they rotate back and forth: I call them to the front of my mind to solve a particular design problem. It is a kind of a language—or rather a vocabulary, but people read it as language. People say, "Well, if it's plaster and has color, then it is in the style of Legorreta." This is a generalization that sometimes disturbs me. I use native materials and color because I like them, but the intention goes beyond just saying, "Use color on a wall."

JM: Which of the elements that we see included in your architecture are most important to you?

RL: To me, the planes are the really important elements because not only do they serve the practical purpose of covering and protecting, they limit and define the space. They receive light and reflect it or use it. Planes provide scale and proportion to a space.

Proportions are fundamental when I design. I even change the kind of pencil or pen I am using to define the planes in order to emphasize proportions. I use a piece of cardboard to check if the planes in a space are in proportion, even if I still have not yet checked the dimensions of the room or the house.

Finally, there is no benefit to creating a beautiful space if you don't consider the light entering it. The light is very important. I learned about this in Egypt. When I saw the temples, I was amazed when I was told they were completely dark inside. What for? Why study proportion if it is going to be completely obscured by the dark? Light was the spirit of Louis Kahn; he said that the wall didn't know about its own existence until the light shone upon it. My architecture is completely filled with light.

JM: You have referred to a fourth element that seems to have more to do with Mexico's culture and roots, and that is mystery and emotion, the poetry of a space, the actual experience in a space.

RL: Yes, the three elements that I have mentioned could be called physical. The other elements are emotional. To me architecture without emotions is not architecture. A space can be beautiful, but if it doesn't raise your spirits, it is not architecture.

I love mystery, not only in architecture but in all of life. I love to discover. I love going to a place without knowing what I am going to do or what to expect. This is very much a part of Mexico, and it still confuses people. Trying to explain Mexico and Mexicans is impossible.

JM: You mean that Mexicans are not very rational?

RL: No, not at all. One of the reasons you have problems judging Mexicans is that you think we are irresponsible. In a way we are irresponsible, in another way we are not. It is a special combination of mystery, surprise, and emotion. For example, it was difficult for me to understand a specific architectural program that I was given once in the United States. The office was supposed to have been 360 square feet. When the clients checked and found that it was not according to the program, I told them, "Look, I don't care if it's 360 or 340 or 400 square feet, what is important is that it came out very well." That is Mexican, and it has its risks—the risk of going all the way with emotion and forgetting about the other elements. But the feeling of peace and humanism is extremely important to me. In modern life, we are exposed continuously to stress. To arrive at a place and find peace is extremely rewarding. If I work 12 or 14 hours a day, then a moment of peace becomes the most creative moment of the day. Those moments are an essential part of my life. You cannot separate architecture from happiness.

JM: I would like to discuss the influence of people such as José Villagrán. When you first became an architect you worked in Villagrán's office. Several articles have referred to the influence he had on your life. But to me, Villagrán is a modernist and a rationalist, and your architecture is not modernist or rationalist.

RL: First of all, Villagrán was a real builder. The reason I went to work in his office was that one day when I was a student, I was walking in downtown Mexico City and passed a building that he designed. Normally you don't care about technicalities as a student, but I started to see the details of the construction—how windows and doors worked to perfection. At that moment I decided to work for him because he was a real builder.

One day I went with him to a construction site.

When we arrived, he said, "This wall is built badly." The worker had the typical answer: "Oh, Mr. Villagrán, the brick isn't made as in the old days." So he called the contractor, and he received the same answer. "Okay," he said. He took off his jacket, rolled up his sleeves, and built three perfect square meters of brick. He showed me that we have to know how to build.

Second, he showed me discipline and punctuality. In a country like Mexico, you have the idea of *mañana*. Fortunately, it is not like this anymore, but at that time architects always took pride in not being punctual.

Third was his passion for the profession; he had respect for his position as an architect and for standing up against forces that could hurt you—corruption, bad authorities, commercialism.

I spent twelve years learning from Villagrán the ethics of the profession and how to work. On the other hand, in his office I was limited creatively; I was not convinced of his design. I liked it, but it was typically modernist; it had no emotion, it was absolutely rational. So when I was ready to explore, I had the knowledge and a sound basis for architecture. When I shouted "¡Viva México!" I had already learned the structure, the philosophy, and the order of architecture from him.

JM: A second name I would like to introduce is Luis Barragán. You were involved in discussions with Barragán during the design of the Camino Real hotel in Mexico City, although with that project the actual design elements were not walls and building but landscape. When were you first introduced to Barragán, and did he influence your architecture?

RL: I was first introduced to him in 1964 at the dedication of the Chrysler plant I designed in Toluca. I said to Barragán, "It is really an honor to meet you, thank you very much for coming. What is your opinion of this place?" He said, "Your architecture is first-class. Your landscape, your gardens are lousy." And he was right, they were lousy. At that moment I admired him very much.

I called him later and asked him to explain what he meant. He said, "Look, you can do more with open spaces than you did at Chrysler. I agree that you want to have your walls clean, but landscape is not only grass." And then we started to see each other and develop a relationship, and one day I asked him to give me some advice on the gardens of the Camino Real hotel.

The main connection with Barragán was the sources of inspiration—the love of privacy, humanism, mystery, and color. I consider Luis a special kind of architect—he never was involved in the real life of an architect. For all of his projects, either he was his own client or the clients were people who truly believed in him and would support his experimentation. The main difference between us was that I decided I was going to design for people, and Luis did not believe in that. Luis believed that if you design a beautiful space, people will understand that space. For him the connection was more human than architectural; he was passionate. This is where Luis helped me. It is very personal, but in leaving the rigidity, functionalism, and intellectualism of Villagrán, I found a man who was completely the opposite, someone who really cared about the moment.

The important aspects for him were the right moment for light to enter a space, the right moment to have tea, to talk, to dream. He was able to stop anything just to spend the day away from the office. He would say, "Today is a beautiful day—why don't we go up into the mountains?" He didn't understand schedules. Under Villagrán or my father this was forbidden—it was almost a sin. Luis gave me this balance and focus. On one side, I had Villagrán, and on the other was Luis, the complete romantic. I am very grateful to both.

JM: But did Luis understand architecture and buildings?

RL: Yes, Luis had pure sensibility. Sometimes he would say, "Ricardo, this is very nice," and sometimes, "It's horrible, I can't stand being here." The other day I was participating in a symposium. The three people who spoke before me were very intellectual and they started to analyze and classify Barragán's architecture. It was so academic that when it was my turn to speak, I said, "Look, my only reaction is that if Luis were in this room, he would laugh at your interpretations."

JM: Several artists and painters have been linked with you and your work: Mathias Goeritz, Jesús Reyes, Pedro Coronel, and others. Which artists or painters have influenced your architecture?

RL: I can add somebody else. I never met him, but I have studied him and this has helped me: Louis Kahn. He is one of the architects who really understood roots in the right way—by designing buildings that really belong to a place rather than those that simply impose one's own culture or architecture. Louis Kahn was able to handle everything—circles, planes, straight lines, concrete, brick, site. He influenced me more through his attitude than through his buildings. He also influenced my relations with artists. When young people say to me, "Why does it have to be?" I think of Louis Kahn and say, "The only architecture is one of beauty and honesty."

JM: And the influence of painters?

RL: I do not consider myself an expert, but painting interests me. I see a painting, and there is something I can feel. In particular, the painter that interests me the most is a Mexican, Pedro Coronel. First, he was completely free in his use of color. There was no color scheme in his paintings. In addition, his sense of scale was overwhelming. He loved to paint huge paintings for huge spaces.

A great painter, whom I did not meet, was José Clemente Orozco. Frank Gehry once told me that the only painter who really understood architecture was Orozco. He understood it as part of life and painting. A third painter who influenced me is De Chirico. He handled mystery, depth, and color masterfully. Those landscapes and arcades that go on forever are inspiring.

JM: In the last four years you have introduced your son Víctor into the office. How did this develop, and has it resulted in changes in the office?

RL: This is a very important part of my life. When my daughter Lourdes studied architecture, I was very happy. So when Víctor, who had previously expressed no interest in it, suddenly said, "I want to be an architect," everybody told him not to be an architect. They said, "It's a very difficult profession, and you have Ricardo, an extremely strong personality; he's going to overpower you." But Víctor decided anyway. He went through school without showing me his work. I continually told him to take advantage of me. After he graduated, he worked for a time with Fumihiko Maki in Japan and with Oriol Bohigas in Spain, and went to Orange County, California, to learn about computers in architecture.

One day I said to him, "Víctor, I have to complete the presentation for the children's museum in Mexico City. Why don't you bring your friends to help me?" It was a success. Víctor and his friends came when I presented the project to the wife of the president of Mexico, and she said, "It's beautiful, we approve it." At that moment, to my surprise, Víctor said, "We have something else to show you." They came out with T-shirts, embossed with the logo of the museum, and I thought, "This is great," and the client liked it. So I said, "Víctor, what we have to do is change the office. Why don't you bring your friends and join the office, and we old people will stay in the background." I am always looking for new ideas and new experiences. I don't believe in age calculated in years. Víctor accepted this offer, and since then I have been the happiest person in the world.

Víctor and I don't have any arguments, even about design. You could say, "Well, you don't have any arguments because you, Ricardo, are the one who makes decisions." But this is not true. We have not had any because he is open to learning, and I am open to change, to exploring new directions.

There is another person who has been a definite influence in my life: Noé Castro, my partner. He is an unbelievable person. Through the years he has guided me all the way from conceptual design to welding beams. He will say to me, "Ricardo, you're taking on too much work." When I spoke with Noé about Víctor and his young friends joining the office, he said, "Ricardo, you are right, this is what we have to do. Do it."

JM: Your office has been open now for at least thirty years. What design changes have you seen taking place in your office over that period of time that are important in your work?

RL: Regarding attitude?

JM: Or the end product, the architecture or the building.

RL: Basically, there have been two changes: first, we have tried to be freer with ideas, to have true freedom in creating, thinking, doing. Second, we are trying for something we have not yet achieved: perfection in architecture. This is very difficult in Mexico, because architecture is built with a certain amount of improvisation. You cannot say, "I want this line to be perfect," because then it is artificial. To create a building in Mexico that really works, that you can really maintain, that responds to a budget, is an obvious objective. Our basic law is the constant idea of doing the best we can.

JM: Is there a direction or philosophy that is absolutely critical to your architecture?

RL: I am at an age—I call it the second teenage—at which I realize that there is no "What is it all about?" One option is to tell myself, "I have a reputation and a personal signature or direction, so I can continue doing this and die peacefully." The other is to say, "Look, I am in the best years of my life, and I really want to keep progressing." That has been very important for me; more and more I think that I would like to enjoy life. I do not want to be remembered just as somebody who completed a certain number of beautiful buildings; I want to be remembered as somebody who truly served architecture. To follow that famous phrase of Gropius: "Keep working as if you were going to live forever because if your goals are good, somebody will pick up your flag and keep progressing." To me the joy of life is creating, to be able to continue.

JM: Is there a specific building or space you have designed in which you feel that you actually achieved the kind of magic or perfection that you intended?

RL: Yes and no: I haven't achieved perfection, but in some of my spaces I have achieved a feeling of magic, the feeling that I am moving in the right direction, and in those moments I decide to keep working forever.

LEGORRETA ARQUITECTOS OFFICE

Mexico City, 1966

Located on a steep hillside site on the outskirts of Mexico City, the building hugs the slope as it steps down the hill, adapting to the land.

The objective was to create an unconventional and inspiring working environment completely isolated from the surrounding city. A series of external and internal stairs, patios, and walls connects the spaces and terraces and provides a continuous experience. With the greatest emphasis on space devoted to the design process, the building is less an office than a serene, intimate environment in which to create.

From the selection of the site to the last design detail, the architect developed a sanctuary as a creative oasis insulated against the stresses of the everyday world.

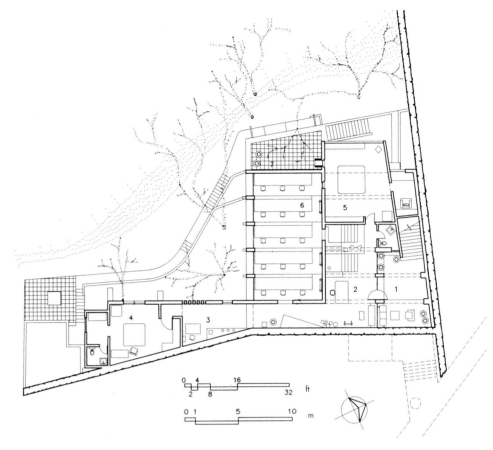

Ground floor plan

1. Entry
2. Reception
3. Secretary
4. Direction
5. Meeting room
6. Design workshop

Left: Entrance vestibule

Opposite: Front entrance

26

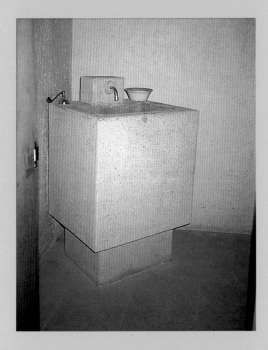

A series of patios and walls connects both interior and exterior spaces to create an intimate working environment sheltered from the street. Simple shapes and natural materials emphasize serenity.

Above: Bathroom details

Right: Meeting room

Opposite: Entrance terrace

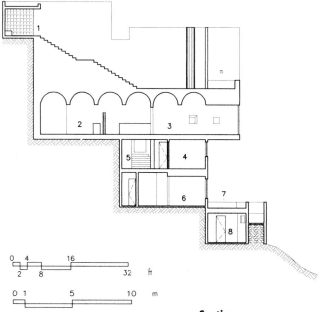

Section

1. Entry
2. Reception
3. Meeting room
4. Private
5. Stairs
6. Private
7. Terrace
8. Office area

"We are a group of friends devoted to creativity who needed the right environment. Hills, walls, and color gave us what we needed."

R.L.

CAMINO REAL MEXICO HOTEL

Mexico City, 1968

The client's initial idea for this site adjacent to Chapultepec Park was a complex of modern high-rise buildings, conventional and undistinguished. A hotel seemed like the ideal use for the site. Legorreta, reacting to the coldness and unfriendliness of most hotels, decided to imbue this design with a unique personality and the feeling of true Mexican culture that would evoke a Mexican home.

A study of bearing walls and the effect of earthquakes on buildings in Mexico City resulted in a maximum reasonable height of five stories. This height accommodated the required number of guest rooms and public spaces with open spaces between them, as well as integrating with the urban environment.

The design shields the hotel interior from the hustle of major streets on three sides but connects with the life of a small shopping street on the fourth side. The building is thus a sanctuary that provides privacy and peace for its occupants. On one side, a bright yellow arcade edged with trees connects the interior public retail activities with the street. The wall is broken on the main street facade by a shocking pink screen. The visitor enters through this screen into the tranquil environment of a motor court that is visually dominated by an oversize fountain. One then passes from this calming enclave into the spacious lobby.

The generously proportioned public spaces invite circulation. Space flows around grand staircases. The architect left the large spaces empty and concentrated user interest in the corners, which are activated with minimal furnishings to appeal to the human scale. Space is the luxury of our time.

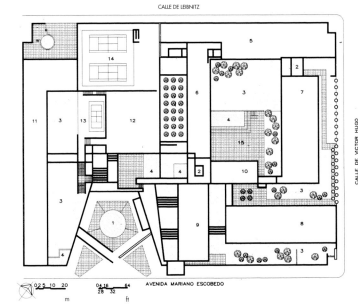

Site plan

1. Fountain entry
2. Lobby
3. Garden
4. Pool
5. Mision de la Sal wing
6. M. del Norte wing
7. M. de la Palma wing
8. M. San Fransisco wing
9. M. Santa Ana wing
10. M. de Capistrano wing
11. Suites
12. Heliport
13. Paddle tennis
14. Tennis courts
15. Main courtyard

To revive the pleasure of walking, the design requires that hotel guests walk considerable distances to the guest rooms; the circulation spaces were designed to provide a sense of luxury through manipulation of light, materials, and color. Rough plastered walls, common in Mexican vernacular architecture, lend dignity to the interiors. Guest rooms face either the central court or private patios, gardens, or rooftop terraces.

The exterior courts and terraces were carefully designed to connect indoor and outdoor spaces, as well as to provide places for public use. Each open space offers a different motif, landscape, and activities. These courtyards contain pools or recreation centers (active) and pergolas, gardens, and rooftop terraces (passive).

Right and above: A grand staircase leads from the spacious lobby to a conference center. At the top of the stairs is a mural by Mexican artist Mathias Goeritz.

Opposite: Guest rooms face either the central courtyard, shown here, or private patios, gardens, and rooftop terraces.

Motor court

Suites swimming pool

Presidential suite

Presidential suite

MARCO CONTEMPORARY ART MUSEUM

Monterrey, Nuevo León, Mexico, 1991

The museum design was inspired by the traditional Mexican house plan: a central courtyard edged by an arcade that provides access to the adjacent spaces. This design was then integrated with the urban setting—a key corner of Monterrey's Macroplaza flanked by the cathedral. The museum has become the city's cultural center.

Pedestrian access is through an entry plaza in which sculptor Juan Soriano's gigantic dove pays nostalgic homage to Luis Barragán's pigeon house. From this entry plaza one walks through inconspicuous doors to the vestibule, a tall space with carefully controlled light and color. This change in spatial sequence, from the large entry plaza to small doors, heightens the sense of spaciousness inside. The vestibule provides access to the auditorium, cafeteria, and gift shop. After the visitor passes under a sculptural lattice, he

or she arrives at the main courtyard, which serves as the focal element and access point to all galleries. Periodically a torrent of water flows from a fountain along the wall to cover the courtyard and energize the space. The courtyard also functions as a place for concerts, receptions, and gatherings.

Art exhibitions are displayed in spaces and environments of different proportions, forms, and heights, with strategically situated rays of natural light penetrating the spaces. Carefully placed openings also keep the visitor in touch with the city and the central courtyard without distracting from the exhibitions. The building materials and intense colors complement the informal and elegant building and challenge the curators to take advantage of the natural light, texture, and color. This has resulted in exciting and successful exhibits that challenge artists and attract the public.

Opposite: A giant dove by sculptor Juan Soriano marks the pedestrian entry plaza.

Below: The museum anchors a corner of Monterrey's central plaza and has become the city's cultural center.

Above: The soaring entrance
vestibule with its information desk
provides access to the central
interior courtyard, auditorium,
cafeteria, and gift shop.

Opposite: Strong color and
sculptural forms characterize
the exterior.

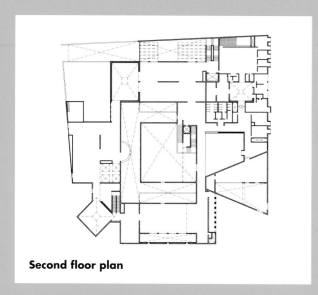

Second floor plan

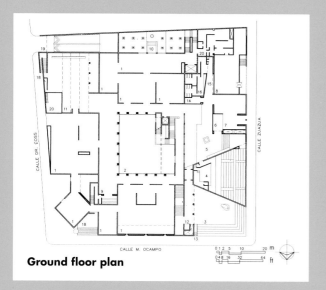

Ground floor plan

1. Exhibition hall
2. Central patio
3. Entrance
4. Auditorium
5. Information
6. Orientation hall
7. Gift shop
8. Restaurant
9. Cafe
10. Sculptural patio
11. Orange patio
12. Ticket booth
13. Handicapped access
14. Cloak room
15. Telephone
16. Public restroom
18. Emergency exit
19. Parking
20. Private areas

"Art should be part of our daily life. Museums should be human and inviting, full of light and color."

R.L.

Above: Inspired by the traditional Mexican house plan, the central interior courtyard is lined with an arcade and is the access point to all galleries.

Opposite: Water alternately trickles and gushes from a fountain in the central courtyard, which is also used for receptions and concerts.

Right: Tall spaces, intense colors, and natural light, as seen in this interior courtyard, complement the exhibitions.

Opposite: A sculptural lattice separates the entrance vestibule from the central courtyard.

EL PAPALOTE CHILDREN'S MUSEUM

Mexico City, 1993

This museum is for and of the Mexican children and symbolizes the Mexican family. Situated at the edge of Chapultepec Park, the children's museum integrates with the fountains and part of the Chapultepec forest. This symbolic connection is carried into the interior courtyard through the use of stone and water. The open and closed spaces are arranged naturally, inviting the visitor to wander as if in the forest. Children are liberated here to gain an interest in discovery and feel as if the museum belongs exclusively to them.

The basic geometric forms—cubes, a sphere, and triangular shapes—are easily identified at a distance and are familiar to children. The variety of forms and spaces also awakens curiosity and retains the visitor's interest during repeat visits. The volumes are defined by shape and color (traditional glazed tiles were used, recovering an ancient Mexican tradition). Natural light, colors, and materials create a cheerful and exciting building and evoke both the character and the culture of Mexico.

The children's museum is a truly humane and joyful building. Its design is dedicated to Mexico's major treasure: its children.

49

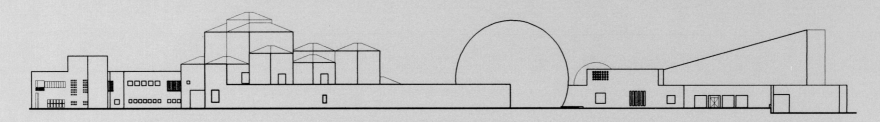

East elevation

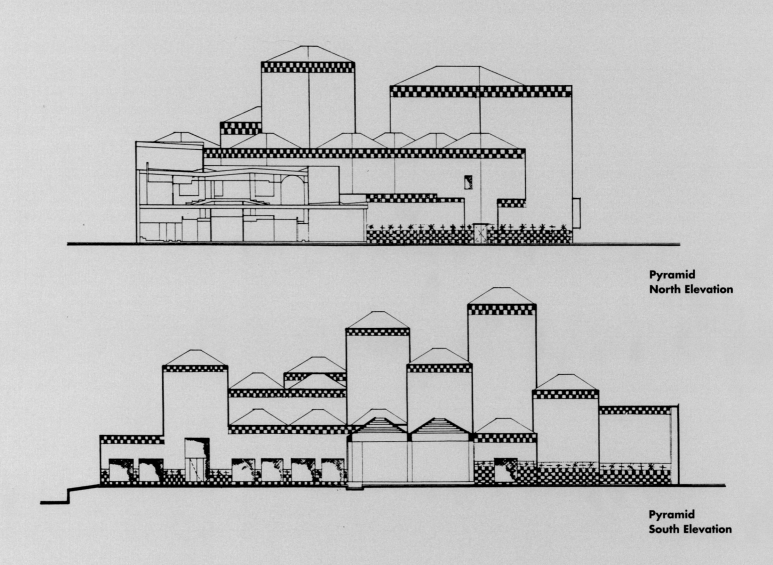

**Pyramid
North Elevation**

**Pyramid
South Elevation**

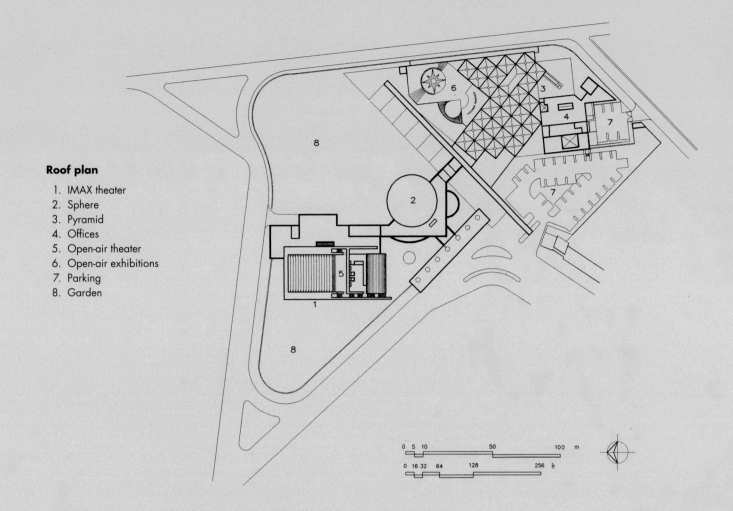

Roof plan

1. IMAX theater
2. Sphere
3. Pyramid
4. Offices
5. Open-air theater
6. Open-air exhibitions
7. Parking
8. Garden

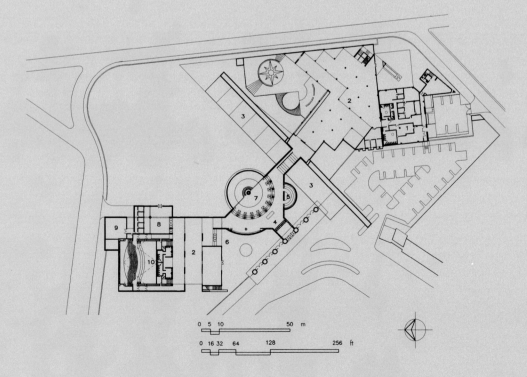

Floor plan

1. Administration area
2. Exhibition
3. Fountain
4. Vestibule
5. Orientation room
6. Main access
7. Sphere
8. Coffee shop
9. Emergency plant
10. IMAX theater

Above: Playful sculptures in the central garden invite visitors to wander as if in a forest.

Opposite: Basic geometric forms and cheerful color define the museum and make it easily recognizable to children in Chapultepec Park.

Above and opposite: Hand made glazed tile on the exterior recovers an ancient Mexican building tradition, while bright color creates a joyful children's environment.

Above and opposite: Natural light, a variety of materials, and free-form displays inside the museum encourage imagination and discovery.

"Children's world . . . .
Happy building full of freedom, dreams,
imagination, and friendship . . . ."

R.L.

CERVANTES HOUSE

Mexico City, 1996

The site for this house is an irregular lot in west Mexico City, with views toward neighboring houses. The design is based on a series of outdoor courtyards and freestanding walls punched with irregular windows and latticelike openings. Stone and marble floors contrast with the rich ochres and earth tones of the walls.

Color plays an important role throughout the house, reflecting light in the interior and in the intimate exterior courtyards. Water also assumes an important but subtle presence in the entry courtyard, where water trickles from a discreet fountain onto a custom-designed stone floor by Vicente Rojo, and in the main courtyard, where a shallow pool extends from a nearly freestanding wall that blocks views of the neighbor's tennis court.

The interior was designed to create an informal, elegant atmosphere, with freeflowing spaces that respond to the needs of a family. Many decorative elements were custom-designed for the house, including wood cabinets, stairs, and latticed doors.

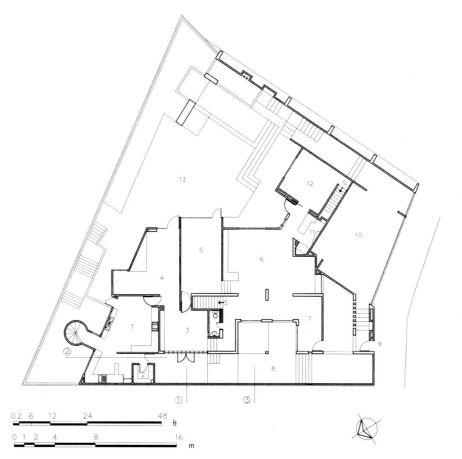

Ground floor plan

1. Kitchen
2. Pantry
3. Breakfast room
4. Family room
5. Dining room
6. Living room
7. Vestibule
8. Courtyard
9. Entry
10. Garage
11. Bar
12. Office
13. Courtyard

0 2 6 12   24   48 ft

0 1 2   4   8   16 m

CAMINO REAL IXTAPA HOTEL

Ixtapa, Mexico, 1981

The site for the hotel was selected literally from a vantage point on the sea, as the client was searching for just the right shoreline along this resort area in the state of Guerrero. Legorreta's design evolved from the land, the imposing sea, the cove, the cliff face, and the rugged mountain range in the background.

Legorreta adapted the hotel to the topography by hugging the building to the cliff face and integrating the tropical vegetation of the site with the architecture. These elements were then used to establish the hotel as its own presence.

The plans then developed naturally. The principal public reception rooms cluster along the crest of the bluff. Guest rooms are terraced to adapt to the slopes, with the terrace of one room forming the roof of the room below as the hotel flows down the hill. The incorporation of nature and life into the project extends into the public areas. The main lobby, lounge, and restaurant open to the natural environment and are not air-conditioned in order to complement the sense of being one with the surroundings.

Three different climates were created in the guest rooms. First, the enclosed sleeping quarters provide the option of air-conditioning or ceiling fans. Second, each room features a covered terrace suitable for dining, resting, or socializing that is separated from the sleeping area by a sliding louvered screen. And third, terraces that extend outward to the Pacific embrace the open air. In each deluxe suite, a private swimming pool on the terrace appears to merge with the ocean and horizon beyond.

As life on the Pacific coast often proves expansive, special treatment was given to the hotel's pool area.

Located at mid-level along the cliff face, the pool area offers a festive variety of walls, aqueducts, and fountains surrounding the sunbathers and swimmers. The beach was left untouched in its pristine state. The design eschews piers and other constructions that might intrude on the land. On the other hand, palapas (thatched palm umbrellas) blend with surf, sand, and the natural vegetation to shield bathers from the sun.

The site recalls the forgotten pleasures of walking and the relaxed lifestyle of Mexico. The cove and bluff are laced with walkways, paths, and stairways for those who wish to stroll, meditate, or wander through the magical environment.

Camino Real Ixtapa is Mexican in spirit, form, space, materials, palette, and furnishings. The ensemble is spacious, romantic, spiritual, and powerful.

Site plan

1. Beach
2. Pool area
3. Access area
4. Sea
5. South building
6. North building
7. Public building
8. Tennis courts

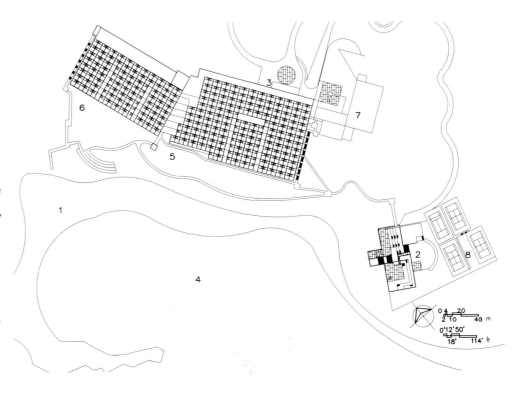

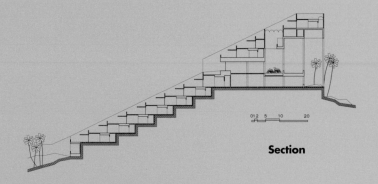

Left: Guest room terraces open to dramatic views of the Pacific Ocean.

Opposite: The hotel hugs the cliff face, with the terrace of one guest room forming the roof of the room below.

Above and opposite: Fountains, a
minimalist "aqueduct," and several
pools create a variety of spaces
for swimming and sunbathing.

Left and opposite: The casual main lobby and public areas open to the outdoors and are not air-conditioned so guests can enjoy the surrounding tropical environment.

Left: Powerful sculptural forms in the entrance portico evoke the hotel's romantic, relaxed Mexican spirit.

Opposite: A winding stone staircase and a concrete elevator tower nestled in vegetation lead to the hotel's pristine cove.

RENAULT FACTORY

Gómez Palacio, Durango, Mexico, 1985

The Renault factory site is a desert. Legorreta initially reacted to the awe-inspiring site: "The desert is magic, it is not possible to describe it; it only absorbs you. I found myself with desert and walls, walls that never end. I did not want to soften this emotion, so instead of landscaping the open areas, we covered the site with cobblestones; instead of a sweet color, we used red. Instead of fighting the desert, we complemented it."

The distribution of the buildings on the terrain corresponds directly to their appointed functions. To connect these functions, the plant is designed about two principal axes, one running from north to south and one from east to west. This provides the best orientation for assembly lines, simplifies the distribution of staff and raw materials, and facilitates the complicated flow among spaces.

Upon entering, the observer is greeted by the Renault symbol, located in the primary access plaza on the north-south axis. A spinal column originates from this plaza and distributes the staff to changing rooms and working places. On the east side of this spine are the main assembly building, engine testing area, research offices, technical reception, and storage areas. A courtyard inserted between the engine testing areas, offices, and assembly areas introduces the external environment and allows future expansion. Along the same axis is a restaurant designed around a courtyard and surrounded by landscaped spaces, providing a visual connection with the environment.

At 500,000 square feet, this complex appears as vast and infinite as the desert itself. The mystery and

desolation of the desert suggested the building's character, which depends on the distinct form of the wall. The approach is dramatic: a long, low wall hovers behind flowing sand dunes. Free-floating exterior walls extend into the desert and become sun screens. Legorreta pays homage to the desert by transforming it into a lawn of stones.

A wall is much more than a linear enclosing element. When thickened, it provides security and thermal mass; when stretched, extruded, or duplicated, it offers shelter from the sun; when punctuated with openings, it provides light, access, and visual connection; when covered in vibrant colors, it radiates. This factory is a multidimensional celebration of the wall.

The vast complex includes an assembly building, testing area, research offices, storage, changing rooms, and a restaurant distributed around two principal axes.

Left: Factory courtyard

Below: Office lobby

Opposite: Office corridor

Above: Natural vegetation and colorful walls celebrate the
surrounding desert.

Opposite: Fountains and pools in the office courtyard offer
a cooling counterbalance to the harsh, dry climate.

TECH HOUSE

Monterrey, Nuevo León, Mexico, 1993

Several years ago, the Monterrey Institute of Technology initiated a biannual raffle. The major prize is a house and a fund for maintaining the house.

For its fiftieth anniversary the institute asked Legorreta Arquitectos to design one of the houses. The program required that the design emphasize the climate, culture, and lifestyle of the citizens of Monterrey.

The initial design statement, a wall, isolates the house from the urban context. The observer penetrates the wall into a courtyard that provides the main vehicular and pedestrian access to the house. Inside the house is a second courtyard, recalling the traditional Mexican hacienda plan, which creates an ambience of intimacy.

The house has two floors with patios and courtyards linking the separate spaces. All of the common family activity areas are on the first floor. The living, dining, and family rooms face the main patio, which includes the swimming pool and landscaped areas. The second floor is reserved for more intimate and private uses. The furniture and landscape were designed by Legorreta Arquitectos.

The exterior is a series of stacked masses and walls, finished in stucco and painted in different tones of yellow and terracotta. Strong colors are used as accents throughout the house.

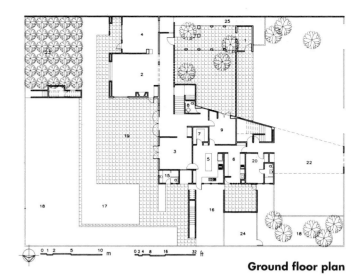

Ground floor plan

Entrance courtyard

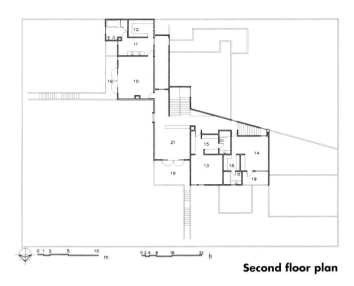

Second floor plan

1. Entry
2. Living room
3. Dining room
4. Library
5. Kitchen
6. Laundry
7. Pantry
8. Powder room
9. Breakfast
10. Master bedroom
11. Master wardrobe
12. Master bathroom
13. Bedroom 1
14. Bedroom 2
15. Bathroom/Wardrobe
16. Recreation courtyard
17. Pool
18. Garden
19. Terrace
20. Maid's room
21. Family room
22. Garage
23. Vegetable garden
24. Parabolic courtyard
25. Reflecting pool

Library terrace

Above: Inside, grilles and
archways recall elements of a
traditional Mexican hacienda.

Opposite: A loggia in the
reception area admits light
and provides a visual link to
adjacent spaces.

Opposite: Legorreta Arquitectos designed the furniture throughout the house.

Right: Sculptures by artist Javier Marin animate a space in the dining room.

MONTALBAN HOUSE

Hollywood, California, 1985

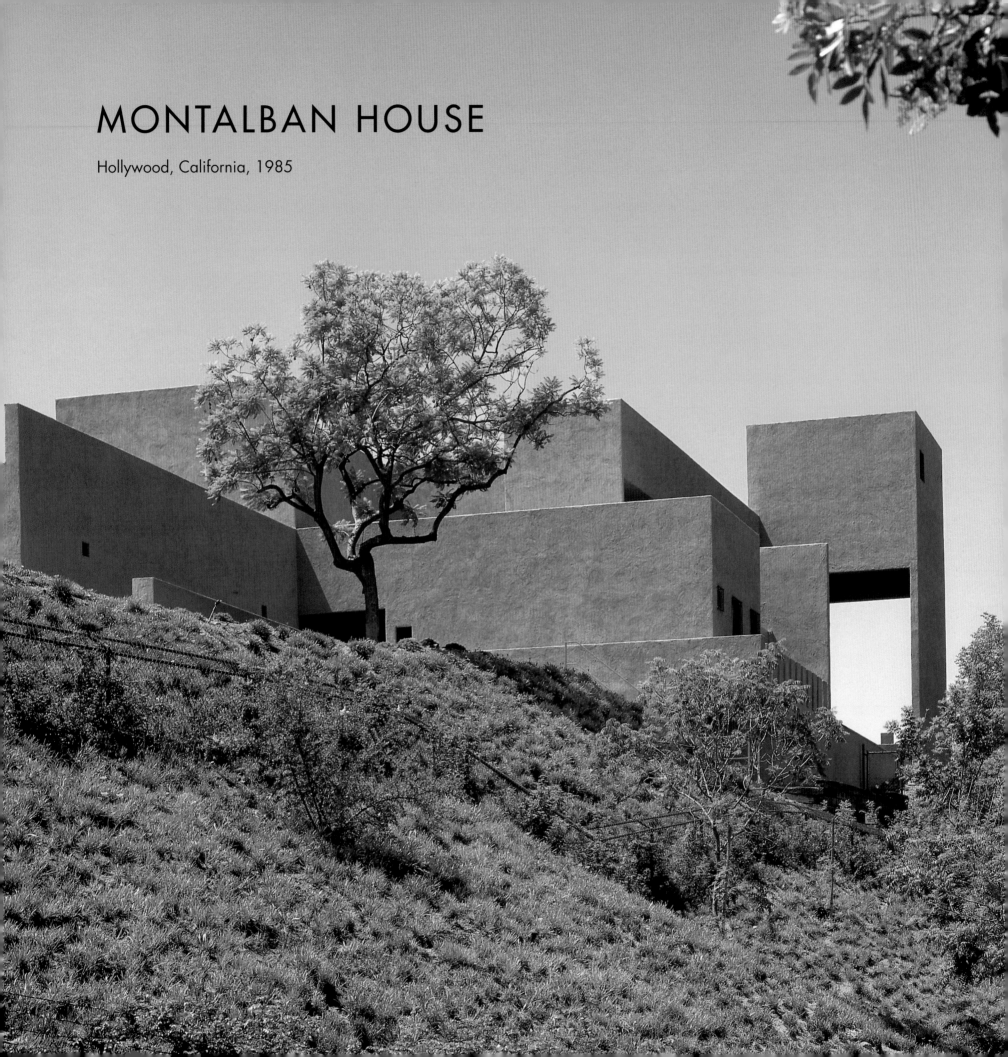

This house, Legorreta's first project outside his home country, represented a specific challenge. It was designed for the Mexican actor Ricardo Montalbán and his wife Georgiana, who requested that the house represent Mexico in the modern sense. The house was also to provide the privacy required by a public figure without being ostentatious.

Located on a bluff in the Hollywood Hills with a spectacular view of Los Angeles, the house evokes a sculpture, a silent series of masses and walls that grow from the earth and engage the blue sky.

The program called for few but ample rooms. An entertainment area for music and television represents the actor's lifestyle, and swimming pools suit the Southern California environment. The reception area was designed to accommodate both a large number of guests and intimate dinners. Floors crafted from Mexican stone run through the house and are covered with handmade carpets in the bedrooms.

The primary walls are finished with rough plaster in an earth tone to form a connection to the ground. In certain areas of the house, bright colors accent significant spaces or volumes. Walls envelop the swimming pool to reinforce its connection to the house and to capture the reflected azure light.

The house emulates the culture and modern lifestyle of the owners in a contemporary interpretation of the vernacular Mexican hacienda.

Right: Walls surrounding the swimming pool connect it to the house and absorb the strong sunlight.

Opposite: At the entrance, walls seem to rise from the ground and provide privacy without ostentation.

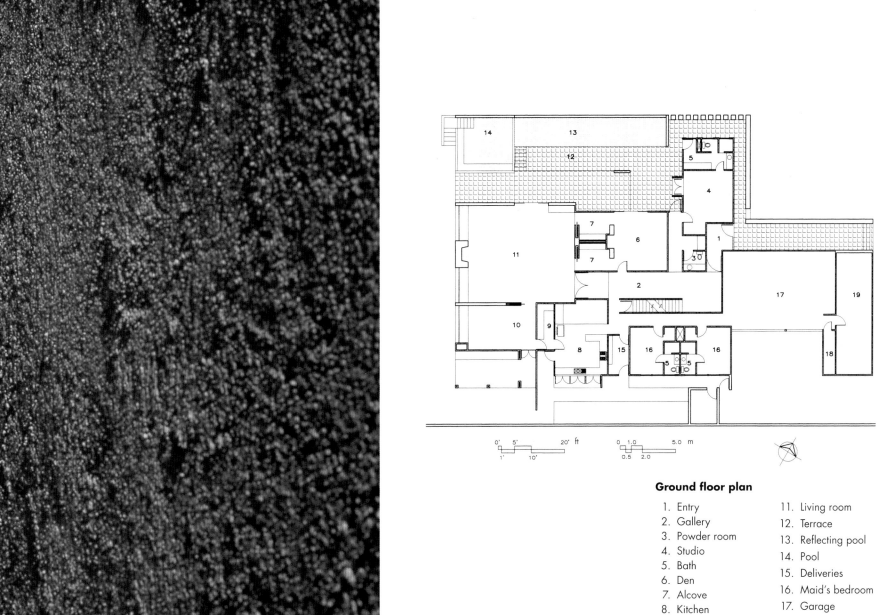

Ground floor plan

1. Entry
2. Gallery
3. Powder room
4. Studio
5. Bath
6. Den
7. Alcove
8. Kitchen
9. Pantry
10. Dining room
11. Living room
12. Terrace
13. Reflecting pool
14. Pool
15. Deliveries
16. Maid's bedroom
17. Garage
18. Dog's run
19. Potting area

"Mexico's presence in Los Angeles

an architectural gift to a great country...

a homage to a great man."

R.L.   93

PERSHING SQUARE

Los Angeles, California, 1994

Pershing Square, located in the heart of Los Angeles, is destined to be an inspiring affirmation of the city's future. With its striking ten-story purple campanile and artistic interpretations of the city's history and culture, this latest incarnation of the 120-year-old park resulted from a collaboration between Legorreta Arquitectos and landscape architect Laurie Olin.

The block was too large to function as a single, symmetrical space, so the designers transformed the square into two spacious plazas linked by the east-west walkway and midblock crossings to the surrounding context. The north-to-south change in level is accommodated along this centerline with a spacious ramp and steps.

The focal point is the 125-foot campanile. At the base of the tower, water flows from an aqueduct into a large, pebble-covered circular pool that dominates the southern plaza. Its timed release causes a tidal action every eight minutes. Artist Barbara McCarren traced an earthquake faultline through the plaza from the pool to the sidewalk, recalling the city's tentative geography.

Two bright yellow buildings connect the southern and northern plazas, the triangular transit center serving bus patrons. The Pershing Square café, overlooking the bustling park, evokes those of European squares. In the northern plaza brightly painted walls of various sizes define spaces and create gathering places. The walls are punctured with squares, rectangles, and circles to frame views in shades of pink and purple. Large, freestanding concrete spheres, a signature of Legoretta Arquitectos, and geometrically arrayed palm trees identify and shape spaces of their own.

The new square is a choreography of elements knitted together to form a lucid yet complex series of spaces. What was once an unfriendly space in downtown Los Angeles has been replaced with an open space that recaptures the lost opportunity of community and contemplation.

"Architecture should serve society, creating spaces for people of all races, giving them the pleasure of walking, reading, meditating, and conversing."

R.L.

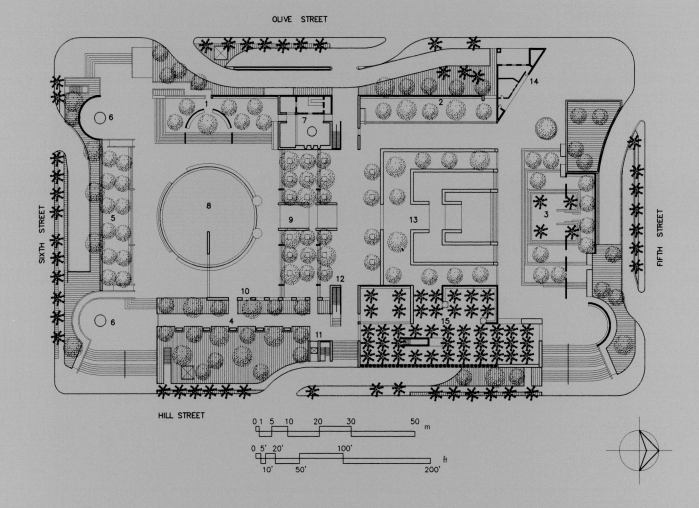

OLIVE STREET

1. Bosque 1
2. Bosque 2
3. Bosque 3
4. Bosque 4
5. Bosque 5
6. Kiosk
7. Pavilion
8. Fountain basin
9. Orange court
10. Aqueduct
11. Elevator tower
12. Tower
13. Amphitheater
14. Transit stop
15. Palm court

SIXTH STREET

FIFTH STREET

HILL STREET

0 1 5 10   20   30   50 m

0 5' 20'   100'
10'   50'   200'   ft

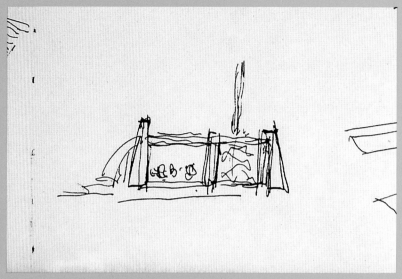

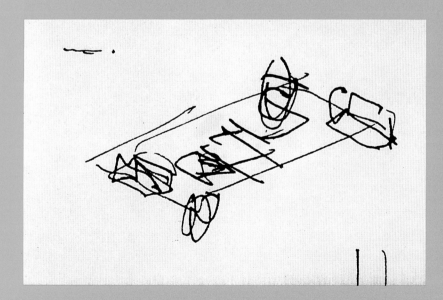

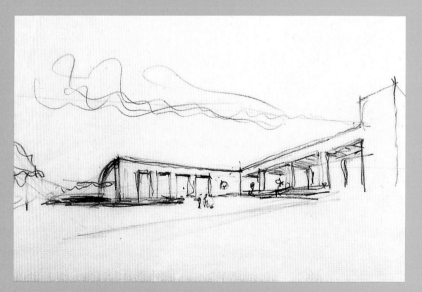

RANCHO SANTA FE HOUSE

Rancho Santa Fe, California, 1987

The house occupies a magnificent site overlooking the Santa Fe Valley. Created as a second home for a successful businessman and his wife, it is now used frequently. The design responds to the owner's personality and provides an elegant, simple, and peaceful place for family life.

Legorreta initially conceived a structure that would blend into the landscape and appear as a wall on the crest of a hill, enveloping the house.

The climate and the owner's lifestyle called for an extensive outdoor living environment, so terraces, a swimming pool, and a tennis court extend out from the house. Exterior walls take advantage of the natural light and shadow and are framed with water and color.

The residence was designed as two houses that operate separately, linked by an element that has since evolved into a galleria. The galleria and the main living spaces incorporate old beams and doors made of rough wood, exploiting the contractor's interest in working with old wood.

Each room exudes its own personality. This allows the family members to enjoy different experiences as they move from room to room throughout the house. Views, light, color, and their effect on space were carefully planned and controlled to create a sense of mystery and enhance enjoyment. Space and light also create an environment for art works.

Above and opposite: A massive entrance wall blends into the landscape and envelops the house, hiding it from the valley below. Terraces and natural materials respond to the owner's outdoor lifestyle.

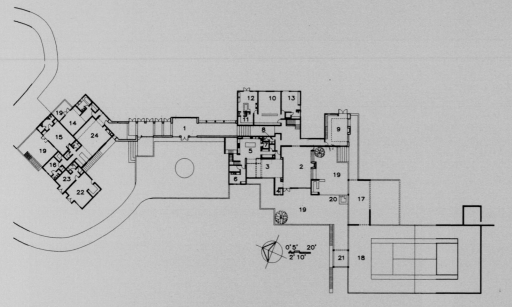

Ground floor plan

1. Entry
2. Living room
3. Dining room
4. Bar
5. Kitchen
6. Laundry
7. Pantry
8. Powder room
9. Library
10. Master bedroom
11. Master wardrobe
12. Master bathroom
13. Exercise room
14. Bedroom 3
15. Bedroom 4
16. Bedroom 5
17. Pool
18. Tennis court
19. Terrace
20. Jacuzzi
21. Gazebo
22. Caretaker's living room
23. Caretaker's bedroom
24. Recreation room

Left: Master bathroom

Below: A galleria links the two halves of the house and incorporates old wood beams and doors.

Opposite: In the vestibule, space and light create an environment for displaying art.

SOLANA

Dallas, Texas, 1991

The pastures, oak groves, and rolling hills of Westlake and Southlake provide the context for Solana, an ambitious mixed-use development and office park. In its natural state, Solana's 1,600-acre site is mostly prairie to the southwest, with clearings punctuated by groves of oaks on the northeast. A group of architects was selected to design the individual buildings, including Legorreta Arquitectos, Mitchell Giurgola, Barton Meyers, landscape architect Peter Walker, and Maguire Thomas. IBM required that the design avoid the semblance typical of office parks (a sense of isolation, lack of cohesion, lack of amenities, sterility).

The two guiding design concepts are Peter Walker's deference to the natural landscape and Legorreta's desire to connect the project with Mexico and the region's history. The master plan was to retain the existing native growth, recovering the original prairie. A special entry court, underpass, and various compounds achieve unity through the interplay of the scale of exterior walls, color, and fenestration. Stucco unifies Solana's diverse colors and impressive forms. This ensures an overall unity for the project while offering each architect freedom in the design of individual buildings.

Vertical elements create directional and entrance symbols, and careful use of walls, textures, and colors humanizes the almost unlimited scale of the Texas prairie. The projected build-out for Solana is 7 million square feet, of which 1.3 million has been built, mostly occupied by IBM.

The entry court at the intersection of the state highway and Solana's main artery is marked by a square of red stucco walls, accentuated by a tall, purple triangular pylon standing in a pool of water. This court, radiating brilliance and serenity, offers the visitor's first glimpse of Solana.

The Village Center, also designed by Legorreta Arquitectos, lies across the highway from the IBM complex, and incorporates a Marriot Hotel, two speculative office buildings, a sports facility, and several restaurants. Again Legorreta refers to the Mexican vernacular with a colonial-style plaza, around which

Opposite: The striking building shown here marks the Village Center, composed of a Marriot Hotel, two office buildings, a sports facility, and several restaurants and shops.

Below: The buildings of the Village Center cluster around a plaza, recalling the vernacular style of Mexican colonial villages.

cluster the hotel and white and brown office buildings, supported by the retail center.

These brilliantly colored stucco buildings are unified by the white limestone that edges the punched openings in the walls. Secondary courtyards are more loosely defined, and slanting wing walls connect the architecture to the landscape. Architectural elements, such as a broken freestanding wall, interconnect one building to the next or form edges between the natural landscape and the architecture. The result is a village in which sun, shadows, and trees invite users to walk and socialize.

Beyond is Legoretta Arquitectos' IBM National Marketing and Technical Support Center, an oblique cluster of six low, sand-colored buildings, interconnected along a central spine and arranged around a series of courtyards. The center consists of 35,000 square feet of offices, dining area, and computer center.

The public entrance is through a dramatically lit, barrel-vaulted vestibule whose sandstone floor contrasts with the saturated blue walls and vault.

Employees enter from the parking structure through a long, bright yellow colonnade, with oversize columns and a shocking pink screen wall. In the courtyards, arcades and vibrantly colored screen walls bounce light into the work spaces. The landscaping is laid out in geometric and symmetrical patterns with channels of quiet water.

Opposite: A tall purple pylon and a reflecting pool mark Solana's entry court off the state highway.

Below: Village Center office building

Above: Native prairie growth surrounds the Marriott Hotel in the Village Center.

Below: Hotel entrance fountain

Right: Hotel courtyard

Left: At the IBM National Marketing and Technical Support Center, the public entrance is through a brilliantly colored, barrel-vaulted vestibule.

Below: Office buildings cluster behind a massive vehicular entry tower at the IBM center.

Opposite: A long colonnade connects the employee parking structure to the entrance of the IBM center.

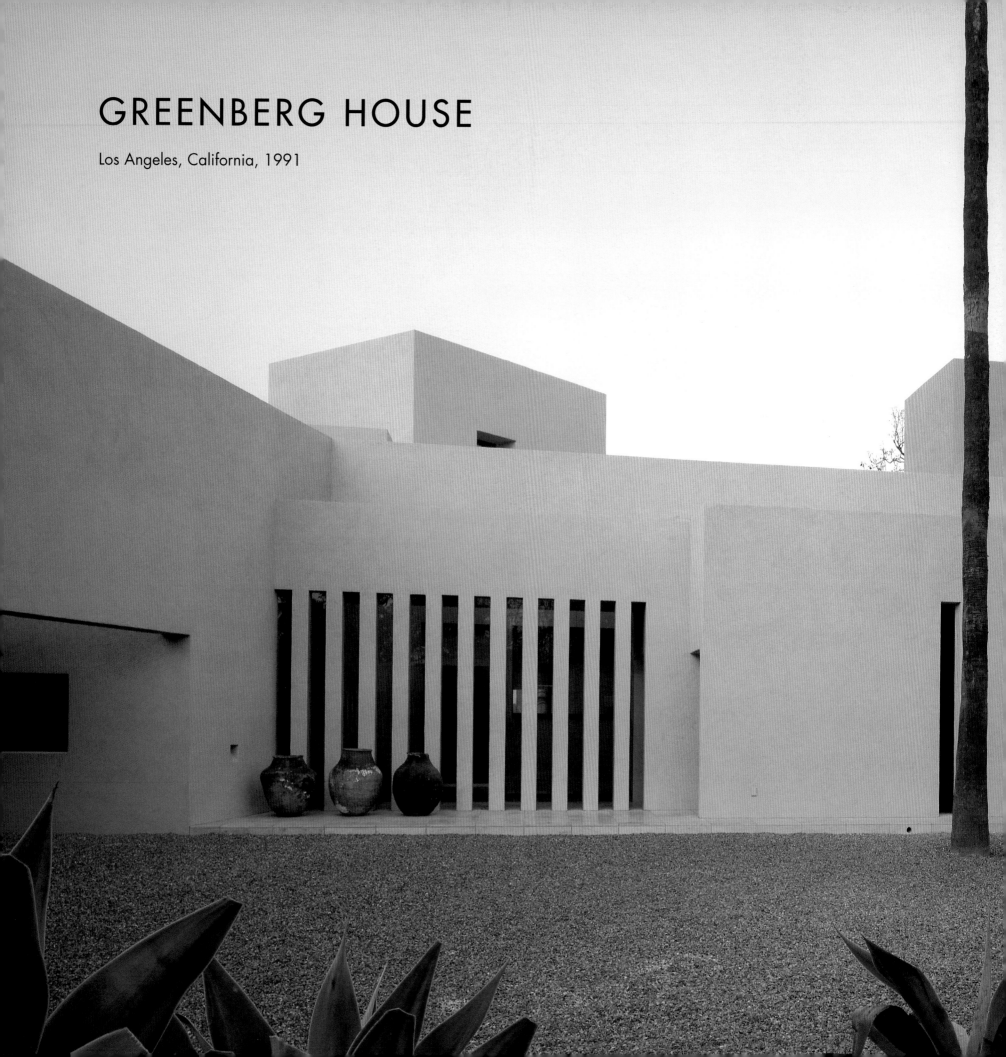

GREENBERG HOUSE

Los Angeles, California, 1991

Located in a residential district of Los Angeles, this house was designed to create its own environment, a vision of architecture as refuge.

The house presents a minimal facade to the street. A motor court edged with walls of different angles and heights in shades of sand, mustard, and bright yellow plaster is set off by a box of river-washed pebbles that cover the court. (Legorreta used a similar element previously as the primary landscape feature at the Renault factory.) The house's asymmetry is emphasized by the minimal landscaping, a group of palm trees and yucca plants. One enters through a courtyard to an unobtrusive front door.

The private side of the house is arranged around two towers, one containing the studio and one, rotated 45 degrees, containing the library. The towers edge, reinforce, and enhance an open terrace. Between them are the primary daytime spaces, living room, and gallery. Below, the pool and jacuzzi complete the interplay of volumes and colors.

With different types of windows, patios, and colors, each room radiates a unique atmosphere. Skylights cast streams of light on hand-troweled walls. Throughout the house, a Legorreta trademark is visible: the everchanging play of light and shadow on walls, heightened by the integration of water and color.

Entrance courtyard

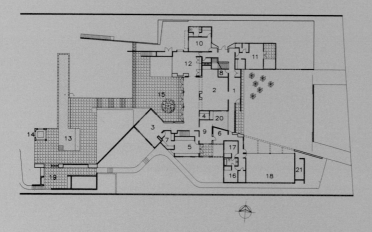

Second floor plan

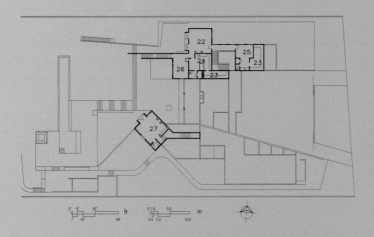

Ground floor plan

1. Entry
2. Living room
3. Dining room
4. Bar
5. Kitchen
6. Laundry
7. Pantry
8. Powder room
9. Breakfast room
10. Bedroom 1
11. Bedroom 2
12. Family room
13. Pool
14. Jacuzzi
15. Terrace
16. Maid's bedroom
17. Maid's living room
18. Garage
19. Covered terrace
20. Reflecting pool
21. Storage
22. Master bedroom
23. Master wardrobe
24. Master bathroom
25. Exercise room
26. Studio
27. Library

Right: The house's two main towers, seen here from the garden, contain a studio and library.

"Two months after they moved in, my friend and client said to me: 'I sleep much better in this house.'

It was the best compliment I have ever received. . . ."

R.L.

PLAZA REFORMA
OFFICE BUILDING

Mexico City, 1993

Plaza Reforma, a speculative office complex, is located in a new development zone on the outskirts of Mexico City.

The primary access for cars and pedestrians is through a square forecourt containing a fountain, a porte cochere, and a tall purple tower marking the axis of the building.

The offices consist of five separate buildings, each offering a unique form and image. The plan allows the building to be occupied by one or several tenants. The design exploits natural light and views of the spacious gardens and private courtyards. Each block is connected by a circulation route containing elevators, stairs, and services.

This architectonic solution provides the complex with an elegant environment and ensures optimum working conditions for the occupants.

The complex is full of vibrant colors and playful shapes and spaces, quintessentially symbolic of contemporary Mexican architecture.

1. Office building A
2. Office building B
3. Office building C
4. Office building D
5. Office building E
6. Central building
7. Entry
8. Fountain

Left and opposite: A square entry forecourt with a fountain and porte cochere is the access point to the five separate buildings in the complex.

"Many hours in the office require a humane and peaceful environment."

R.L.

Right: Meeting room at
AMRO Bank office

Opposite: Typical circulation
corridor

Right: Private courtyard

Opposite: Terrace at
AMRO Bank office

HOUSE IN SONOMA

Sonoma County, California, 1993

Sonoma has soul. Its rolling hills, light, and deep sense of amplitude and intimacy call for an appropriate architecture.

The first task was to choose a spectacular but unimposing site in the beautiful vineyard country. The second was to see that the massing of the house be in scale with both the endless landscape and the human requirements of intimacy.

The approach takes advantage of the rolling terrain and is both mysterious and spectacular in a manner that befits the countryside. Inside, life takes place around a human-scaled courtyard. The interior opens on one side to capture a view of the landscape.

The interiors are designed to house an art collection, not as in a gallery but as part of daily family life. The house changes color during the day as well as in different seasons as the walls absorb and radiate varying levels of natural light. Special attention was given to the color and orientation of the walls to take full advantage of the light's transfigurative properties.

The architect also sought to integrate architecture with the environment. New trees and plants were positioned to blend with both the walls of the house and the landscape.

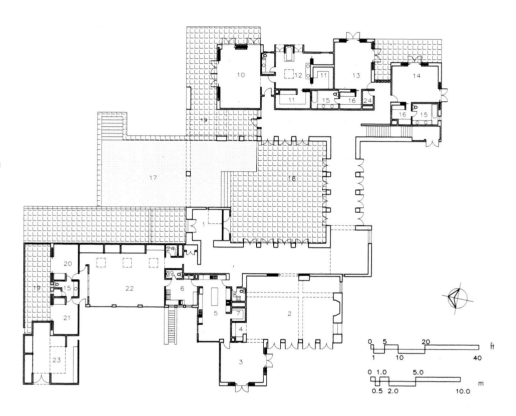

Ground floor plan

1. Entry	13. Guest bedroom 1
2. Living room	14. Guest bedroom 2
3. Dining room	15. Bathroom
4. Bar	16. Wardrobe
5. Kitchen	17. Pool
6. Laundry	18. Center courtyard
7. Pantry	19. Terrace
8. Powder room	20. Maid's bedroom
9. Toilet	21. Maid's living room
10. Master bedroom	22. Garage
11. Master wardrobe	23. Gardener's storage
12. Master bathroom	24. Storage

Above and opposite: Family life revolves around the outdoor pool and courtyard, where the architecture frames views of the rolling hills.

Overleaf: Circular driveway entrance

Right and below: To accommodate the client's art collection, interiors were designed with special attention to wall color and the changing quality of natural light.

Opposite: Olive trees act as sculptural elements to frame the house and blend in with the surrounding landscape.

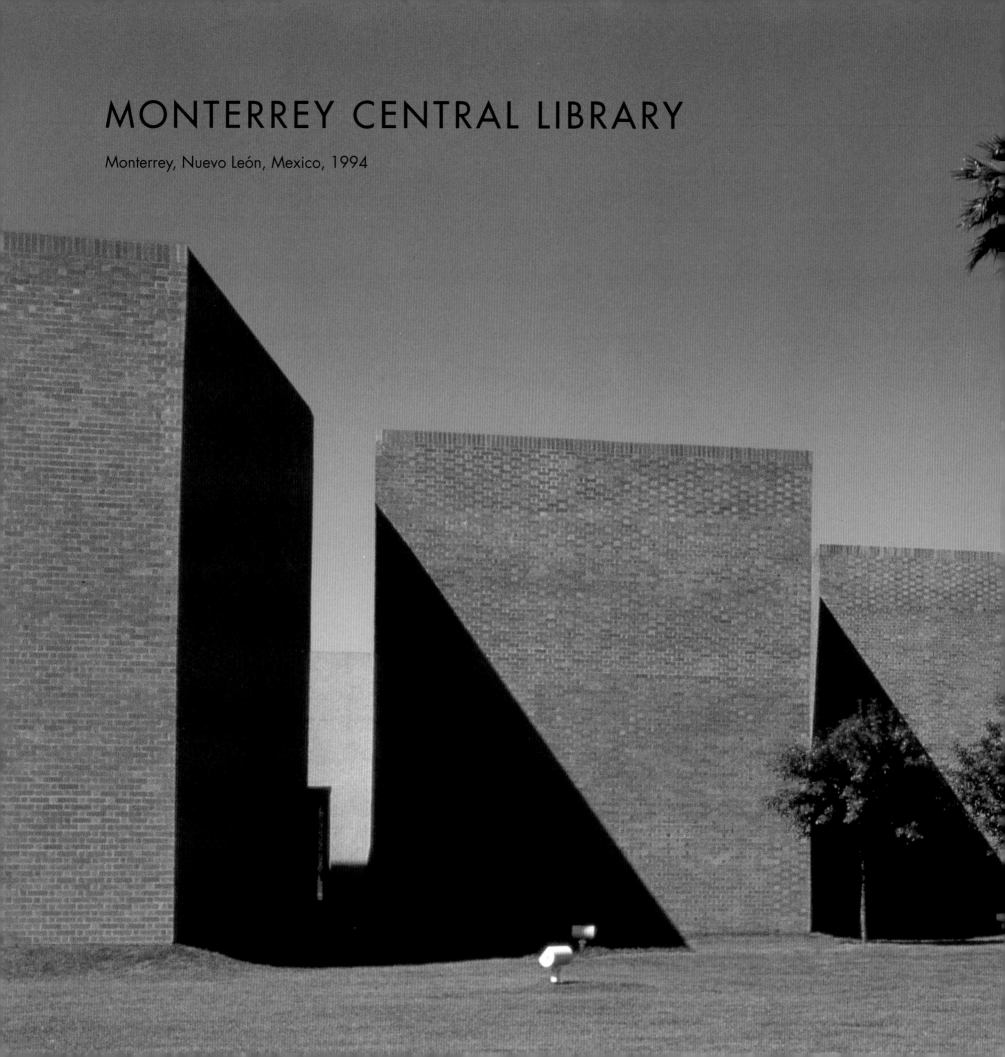

MONTERREY CENTRAL LIBRARY

Monterrey, Nuevo León, Mexico, 1994

Many critical issues impacted the planning and design of the new Monterrey Central Library. The first challenge was to link the building with the adjacent park.

The program required the facility to accommodate two functions: the library serves as the main information center for the university and links via satellite to other educational institutions.

The architect incorporated the nearby lake into the design and siting of the library. Two basic geometric elements, a cube embedded in a cylinder, govern the design. The ends are defined by triangles, one of which descends into the lake, integrating the building with the lake and creating a sculptural effect. Specially designed brick lends color and texture to the cylinder, contrasting with the exposed concrete of the cube and base.

The cylinder and cube house the library's basic functions. The reading areas inside the cylinder feature views of the park. The cube houses the books and is divided into four quarters arranged in a spiral. This divides the floor plan into four platforms, elevated at three-foot intervals. The visual and physical result is a fluid space that provides flexibility in arranging bookshelves and stacks.

A two-story base, designed at a more human scale, contains the administrative areas, auditorium, and Library of Politics. A portico extends through the exhibition galleries in the base and connects the library to University Avenue.

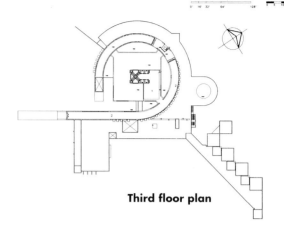

Third floor plan

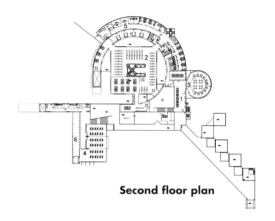

Second floor plan

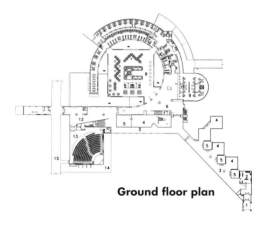

Ground floor plan

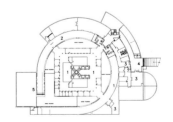

Basement plan

Sixth floor plan　　　**Seventh floor plan**

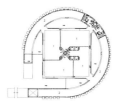

Fourth floor plan　　　**Fifth floor plan**

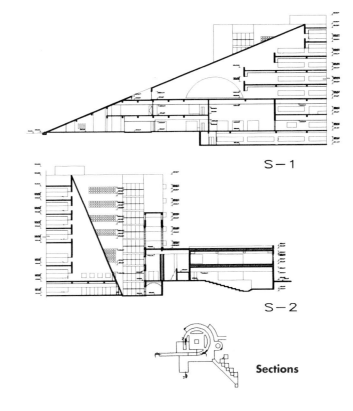

S−1

S−2

Sections

Basement

1. Computer center
2. Administration
3. Service entrance
4. Service area
5. Courtyard

Ground floor

1. Entry tower
2. Bookshop
3. Hall
4. Gallery
5. Courtyard
6. Lobby
7. Reception desk
8. File cabinet
9. Documents circulation
10. Meeting rooms
11. Administration
12. Foyer
13. Auditorium
14. Water fountain
15. Bike path

Second floor

1. Reading area
2. Book shelving
3. Political library
4. Multipurpose room
5. Administration
6. Terrace

Third, fourth, fifth, sixth and seventh floors

1. Book shelving
2. Reading area

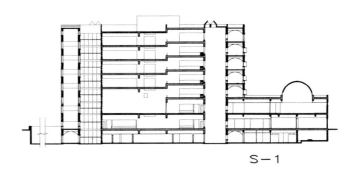

S−1

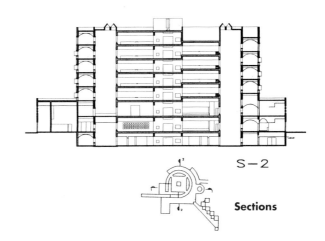

S−2

Sections

"The building is a sculpture in the lake, inviting students to meditate and read by means of beauty and mystery."

R.L.

Above: Rare books reading room

Opposite: Typical reading room

Above: Arched windows in
the reading rooms afford views
to an adjacent park.

Opposite: Access to
meeting rooms and auditorium

Above: Exhibition galleries

Opposite: The cylindrical structure surrounds a cube housing the book stacks, with a skylight illuminating the space between.

BANKERS CLUB

Mexico City, 1994

The new Bankers Club headquarters are located in the historic core of Mexico City in a renovated sixteenth-century courtyard building originally constructed as a girls' school.

The building had suffered severe modifications throughout its life. In the early twentieth century, the building was converted to a theater, and two additional glass facades were added in the 1940s. The initial goal for the present restoration was to eliminate additional elements that proved detrimental to the building's integrity. One facade was restored based on information about its original design. A second facade was left in its modified state, as no such information was available.

A new structure was built on a vacant lot adjacent to the original building. This new building contains all facilities that could not logically be installed in the colonial structure, such as parking, kitchens, health spa, and banquet hall. The facade is contemporary yet harmonious with the historic building.

Pedestrians and cars both enter through a spacious court to the interior motor court and pedestrian hall. The hall leads to the focal point of the building, a central courtyard that has been converted to the main dining room. Four square skylights were installed above, and the stone floor was acquired from an old hacienda.

A colonnade surrounds the courtyard and serves as the principal circulation path, connecting the bar and exhibition gallery with the courtyard. On the second and third floors, additional colonnades provide a visual connection back down to the courtyard and access to private dining rooms and recreational facilities. Contemporary doors, windows, and furniture complete the concept that a building can be modified over time without losing its character.

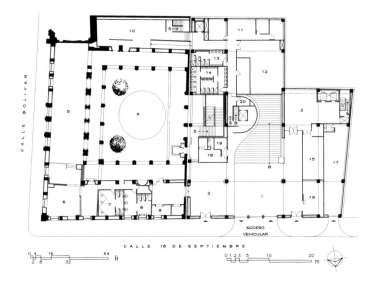

1. Motor lobby
2. Vestibule
3. Reception
4. Main dining room
5. Bar
6. Gambling room
7. Women's toilet.
8. Men's toilet.
9. Cloak room
10. Kitchen
11. Offices
12. Storage room
13. Women's dressing room
14. Men's dressing room
15. Equipment
16. Equipment
17. Motorcycles
18. Chauffeurs
19. Storage room
20. Security

Above: This sixteenth-century courtyard building was severely modified over the years; a photograph taken before restoration shows glass facades added in the 1940s (top). Legorreta Arquitectos renovated the interior (middle), restored one facade to its original design (bottom), and built a new structure adjacent to the original building.

Opposite: The central courtyard is now the main dining room, with four new skylights and contemporary furniture.

Above and opposite: A colonnade surrounds the courtyard, connecting it with the bar and exhibition galleries.

Above: Interior motor court and pedestrian foyer

Opposite: This transition from the new building to the original building successfully blends bright contemporary colors and door fixtures with traditional wood and old stone.

"Remodeling a building requires one to be humble,

recognizing others' talent and completing their job...."

R.L.

CITY OF THE ARTS

Mexico City, 1994

The City of the Arts is a campus that assembles the various national art schools. Before construction, the schools were dispersed throughout the city. On the new campus, each school will benefit from common facilities, including theaters, a multimedia center, a library, and research centers, along with increased interaction among the schools. A second objective is to encourage public interaction with the schools and cultural activities held on campus.

The center includes the national schools of dance, drama, visual arts, music, and cinematography, a theater for 500 people, a library, a multimedia center, a restaurant, an administrative tower with offices for research professors, a cinema complex, and a retail area for shops related to the arts.

The site, on the back lot of a film studio, is very narrow and long, and existing buildings for cinema, television, and the School of Cinematography were to be integrated into the project.

Legorreta Arquitectos won the invitational competition for the project. The basic concept of the master plan was to connect all of the schools and campus elements via walkways. Legorreta Arquitectos suggested that other Mexican architects each be invited to design one building on the campus to illustrate the diversity and richness of contemporary Mexican architecture.

Legorreta Arquitectos assigned each school a site, with a set of guidelines regarding density, height limits, and setbacks. Within these restrictions, each architect had complete freedom regarding architectural expression, materials, and color.

School of the Visual Arts

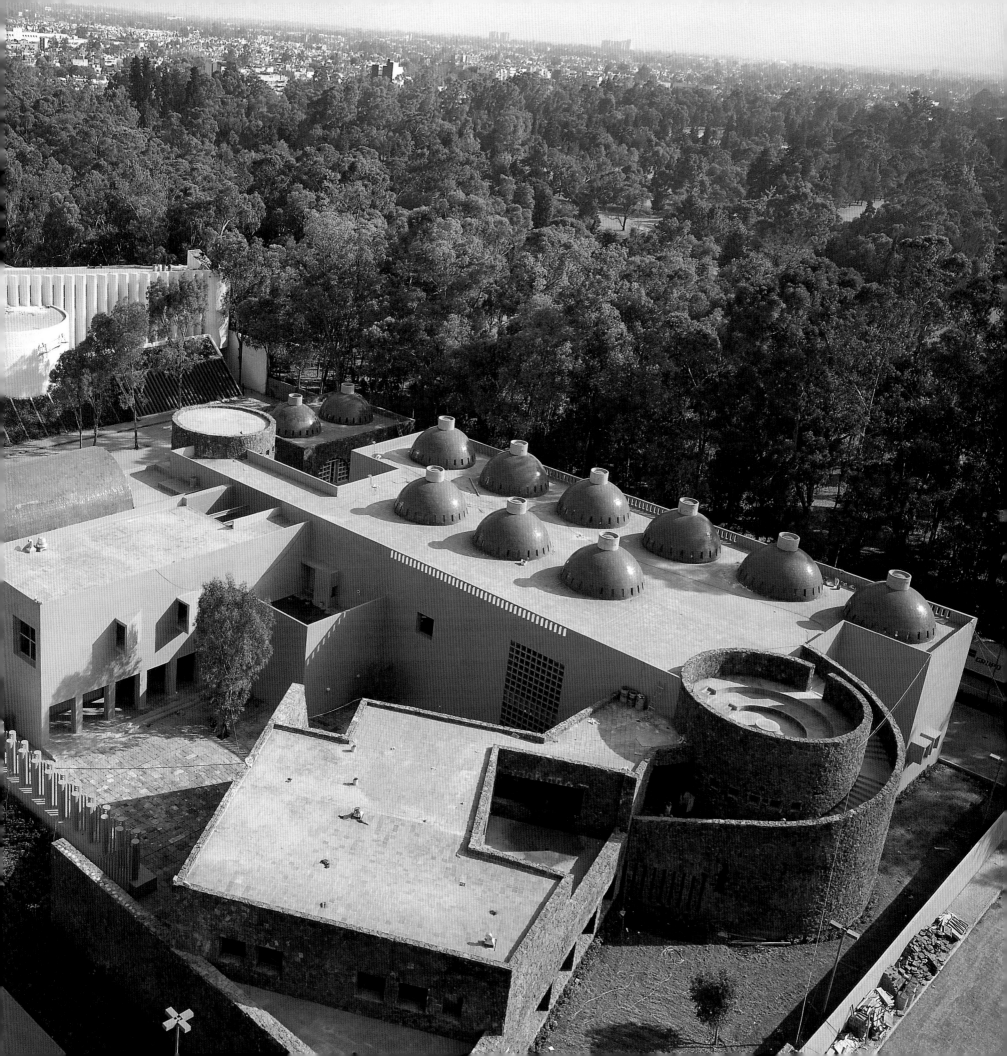

School of the Visual Arts

The school's design found direct inspiration in the ruins of sixteenth-century Mexican convents and the traditional stone walls found in the southern section of Mexico City. Thick walls made out of black volcanic stone combined with walls of color create a series of courtyards and "spaces" that act as classrooms.

In the program, areas for sculpting, painting, textile design, engraving, and photography needed to be able to interact. The plan of the school is flexible and informal, with the option of classes being held in the building, on the patios and the terraces, or in the rooftop amphitheater. Arches, vaults, and domes create spacious interiors, with glass partitions separating the various studios.

Upon entering along a covered colonnade, one approaches the circular studio for life drawing and painting. This studio is wrapped by the primary staircase to the second floor. The entry sequence is constructed out of thick black volcanic stone. The circular classroom is on axis with the three-story sculpture studio, the primary space of the school.

The brick vaults of the painting studios are covered with glazed tile, converting the roof into an outdoor classroom. The result is a Mexican sculpture.

Above: Painting studio

Opposite: Exterior materials incorporate the traditional volcanic stone found in Mexico City's ancient ruins.

Site plan

 1. National School of Drama
 2. National School of Cinematography
 3. Central Building (Library)
 4. Administration and Research
 5. National School of Performing Arts
 6. Theater of Arts
 7. National School of Fine Arts
 8. National Conservatory
 9. Parking
10. Cinema Complex
11. Churubusco Film Studios (Existing building)
12. TV Channel (Existing building)

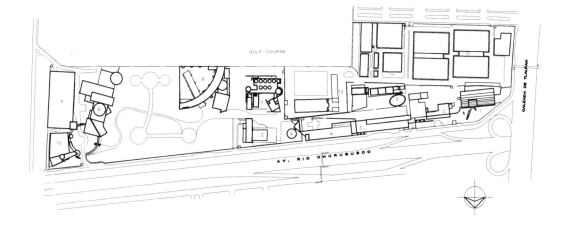

Central Building and Administrative Tower

The primary function of the linear Central Building is to form an axis that links the schools of music, visual arts, and the theater at one end of the campus with the schools of dance, cinema, and drama at the other. A grand staircase and colonnade form the connecting route penetrating the building and linking a series of open porticos with retail space and restaurants on one side and open plazas on the other. In the plazas, open-air concerts, lectures, art fairs, public meetings, and other special events take place. Located in one plaza is an auditorium whose form results from two intersecting vaults. The roof is covered with a tile pattern designed by Mexican artist Vicente Rojo. The long, geometric facade of the main building forms a backdrop to the auditorium, the adjacent campus buildings, and the "art happenings" that occur in the plazas.

The plazas, retail center, bookstore, and restaurant are located on the second floor. On the third floor are the library and the multimedia center, which are used by all of the schools on campus. The library, with its long vaulted ceiling over the reading areas, terminates the three-dimensional form. Parking is provided on the ground floor.

The twelve-story Administrative and Research Tower is located at the end of the long administration building. Designed as a sculptural form based on abstract volumes, it serves as the symbolic center of the campus. The tower consists of two linked volumes: one triangular, which contains the vertical circulation, multipurpose rooms and services; and the second cylindrical, which contains the research centers. Each tower occupies two floors, organized around a two-story space, with administrative offices and meeting rooms on the first level and research offices in the mezzanine.

A detailed study of solar orientation resulted in the exterior projections around the windows, which vary in depth according to location. These solar shades have obviated the need for air-conditioning and cast everchanging shadows on the cylinder.

Right: A staircase penetrates the Central Building and provides seating for casual performances and "art happenings."

Opposite: The Central Building's long colonnade links various parts of the campus and leads directly to the library.

Right: Library in Central Building

Left: Reception area for multi-media laboratories

OFFICE BUILDING IN MONTERREY

Monterrey, Nuevo León, Mexico, 1995

The triangular site generated the building's sculptural plan and massing, while the urban scale carefully addresses the neighborhood. The walls and volumes create patios and terraces on all levels, embracing the building. The terraces have vistas to the mountains; the courtyards create an intimate interior.

The program required two independent buildings within the complex, each with its own identity yet part of the whole. The first is the office for a highly successful and important businessman. A collector of Mexican contemporary art, he requested that his collection be an integral part of the office design. The building was conceived with the atmosphere of an art museum as well as a working space. The building is cubic, with a central atrium providing orientation. The atrium is shifted at each level, allowing natural light to penetrate the interiors.

The second building was designed as speculative office space. Arrival is from the street through a monumental stair leading to the main lobby. The street facade features a series of projecting cubes that cast shadows across the facade and provide protection from direct sunlight. Different colors, selected according to the orientation, lend the building a fascinating palette.

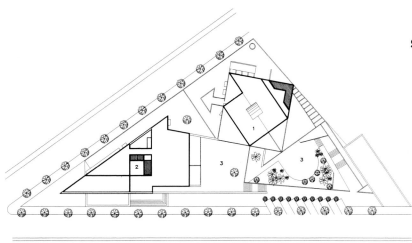

Site plan

1. Office building A
2. Office building B
3. Patio

Above: A central atrium in the cubic building provides orientation and is shifted at each level to allow natural light into the interior.

Opposite: The lobby of the cubic building includes art from the client's collection.

SAN ANTONIO MAIN LIBRARY

San Antonio, Texas, 1995

The City of San Antonio requested a building that the community could celebrate as its own. The program required state-of-the-art technology for information access. The design challenge was to achieve an architecture identifiable as a public building while accommodating the library functions.

Described by local critics as an "ingenious blending of design and function," the new building expands the role that the library is expected to assume. Books remain a critical element, but architecture, art, and technology also received due consideration. The design seeks to entice visitors to discover something new on each visit and thus to attract them back for repeat visits.

The geometry of rotated and cutaway boxes was largely determined by fitting the spatial requirements into the site while generating a friendly and inviting building. The exterior is a visual wonderland of shapes, angles, and openings that create an interplay of light and shadow, both inside and outside. At street level a stone wainscot introduces scale.

A sense of mystery is evoked by blending natural light, shadow, and geometric forms.

The main mass of the library is a six-story box surrounding a yellow skylit atrium that serves as a focal point for each floor. Several terraces are accented by large geometric constructions. Triangular and rectangular baffle walls painted purple or yellow on the third-floor terrace invite visitors to wander outside. The terrace on the west is bordered by a slightly raised water channel that drops into a circular pool. Beyond this channel stands a grove of palm trees.

A sense of freedom was evoked by varying the size and shape of library floors to give each a unique character. Visitors are thus encouraged to discover the building in all of its variety, natural intrigue, and wonder. Graduated child-size stacks are among the unique features of the children's library. Scaled-down furnishings and abundant natural light place young people at ease in an environment tailored to their needs.

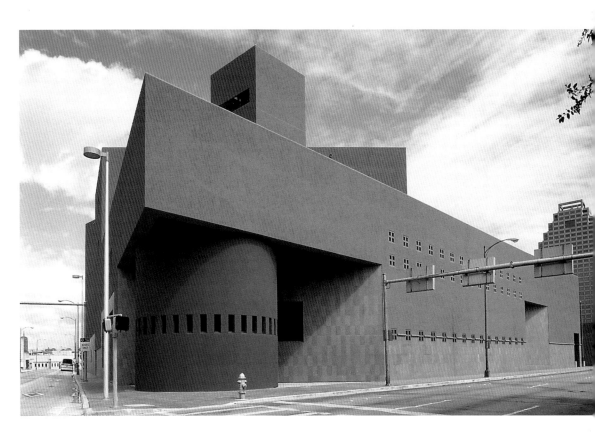

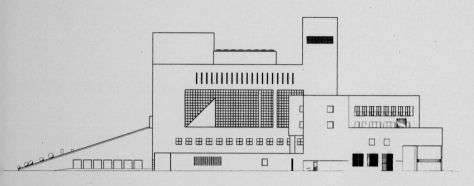

North elevation

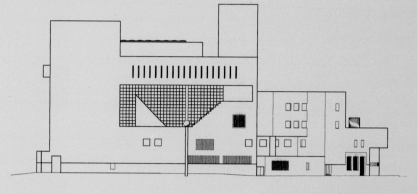

East elevation

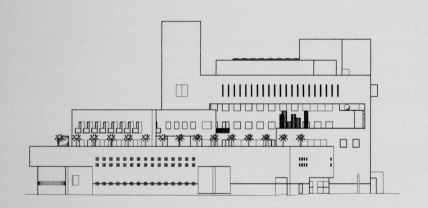

West elevation

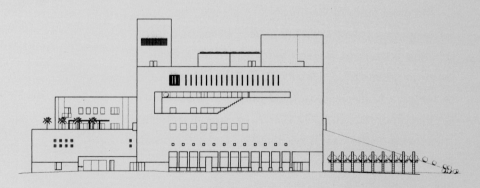

South elevation

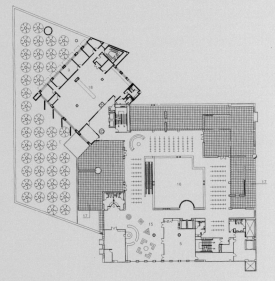

Third floor plan

Sixth floor plan

1. Entry
2. Reception desk
3. Popular library
4. Foyer
5. Multipurpose room
6. Gallery
7. Gift/Book shop
8. Media center
9. Conference room
10. Staff workroom
11. Information desk
12. Reading room
13. Courtyard
14. Periodicals
15. Children's area
16. Atrium
17. Roof terrace
18. Work area
19. Computer room
20. Administration

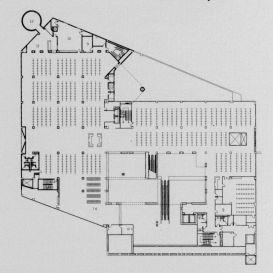

Second floor plan

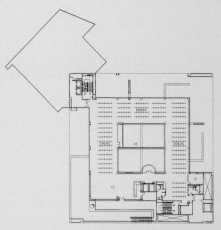

Fifth floor plan

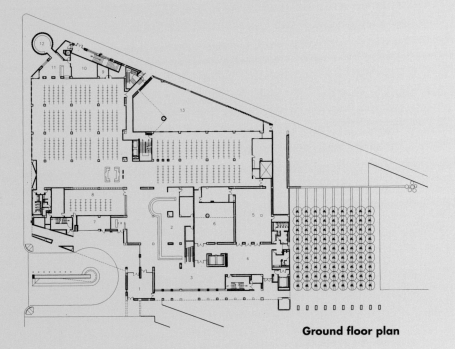

Ground floor plan

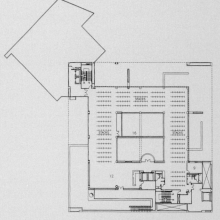

Fourth floor plan

Above: Searing colors, playful geometric shapes, cutouts, and columns create an interplay of light and shadow on the exterior and create a friendly, inviting building.

Opposite: A water channel surrounds the third-floor roof terrace.

Above: The yellow skylit atrium is a focal point for each floor.

Opposite: Abundant natural light fills the reading rooms.

193

LA COLORADA HOUSE

Valle de Bravo, Mexico, 1996

Located on a five-acre site in the town of Avandaro, Valle de Bravo, the house faces south to take advantage of views and sunlight.

One enters through a lemon orchard that ends at a circular motor court. From here stairs lead through a fountain designed as a space of respite before one enters the house.

The interior is articulated longitudinally. The living space, the most important area in the house, is located at the center of this axis and is signaled by an inclined roof with wood beams. Continuing along the axis, one enters the square, double-height dining room.

The entrance and interior spaces generate a continuous experience of light, water, and color, creating different atmospheres for the living space, dining room, bedrooms, and pool area. All spaces open onto views, courtyards, and sky.

The private spaces are divided on two levels: the first level is occupied by the daughters' rooms; the second level is the master bedroom.

The primary pavement material is stone excavated, prepared, and installed by local craftsmen.

Legorreta Arquitectos designed the landscaping and interiors, including the furniture, doors, hardware, and accessories, enhancing the overall ambience and creating a singular design statement.

Opposite: Circular motor court

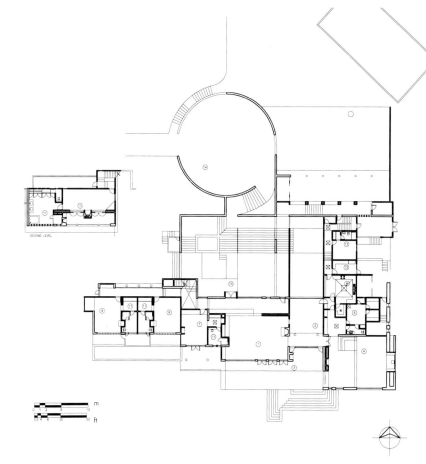

Ground floor plan

1. Living room
2. Dining room
3. Terrace
4. Pool
5. Dressing room/ Pool/Bathroom
6. Kitchen
7. Bedroom 1
8. Bedroom 2
9. Bedroom 3
10. Main bedroom
11. Bathroom/ Dressing room
12. Laundry
13. Maid's room
14. Access patio
15. Access

Right: Front entrance

Below: Stairs lead from the motor court to the entrance courtyard with its stone fountain.

Opposite: A sunny terrace opens off the living room.

CASA JACINTA AND VICTOR

Mexico City, 1996

"In Mexico, we used to say that an architect's worst work is his own house. Maybe it is because you have to deal with the most difficult client of all—your wife— or maybe because in your own house you are free to explore all your ideas and use all the different materials and forms you have seen in your life," says Víctor Legorreta, Ricardo Legorreta's son and partner, who designed this house for himself and his wife, Jacinta.

The idea was to create a series of simple, clean spaces that are classical, not fashionable. The day- time spaces are for working, resting, eating, and entertaining, instead of the traditional formally defined spaces of reception, living room, etc. The house offers different environments without specific uses.

The site, 60 by 100 feet with a steep slope, is located on the outskirts of Mexico City. One enters from the street through a tall, ocher colored wall into the courtyard, which is edged on three sides with walls and on the fourth by the house. This patio is the center of the house. It retains the view of the valley and provides sunlight to the main rooms. Stairs lead to a rooftop terrace, and a fountain set to one side adds the soothing sound of flowing water.

From the patio/courtyard one enters a large room divided by a low wall that creates three environments— the reception/living area, the dining area, and the sunken living room—each with its own character.

The reception/living area looks back onto the patio/courtyard through glass doors and connects the house and the courtyard. The sunken living room/ workplace creates its own predominantly internal environment, with windows placed to accentuate the penetration of light into the space. The dining area focuses on the view to the valley beyond. Light to the interior spaces was a major consideration in the placement of the windows, which look to the patio/ courtyard, to the view at the rear, and to the sky.

The kitchen was inspired by a traditional hacienda and is the detailed focal point of the interior. The ceiling

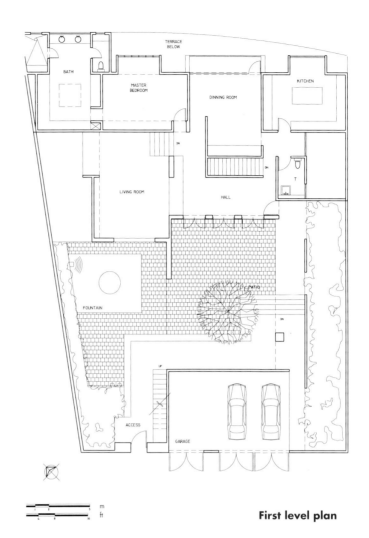

First level plan

and walls are covered with richly colored handmade tiles. The children's rooms and a playroom are on the lower level. The materials are simple in order to enhance the spatial luxury of the high ceilings and large rooms.

The overall design easily accommodates immediate needs: one can change the artwork, the furniture layout, and the uses of each room over time.

Left and opposite: The tall entrance portico leads to the central courtyard, which provides sunlight to the main rooms and is the house's focus.

"I could not describe better my experience working with my father. On the one hand, I have learned the discipline of work, the need to consider details, the effort necessary to make an idea a real building; and at the some time, I have learned the love and passion for architecture and for life.

I have learned from a man who, with incredible generosity, always gives all his heart and effort to every job he gets involved in.

Speaking on behalf of all the young architects now working in the office, I am sure that having worked with my father and architect Noé Castro will leave a big mark on our lives, whatever our futures may be."

V.L.

AKLE HOUSE

Valle de Bravo, Mexico, 1996

Valle de Bravo is a resort area about two hours from Mexico City. A lake was created in this former farming valley when a dam and a reservoir were built to supply water to Mexico City. Akle House, a lake-front weekend house, is only 2,700 square feet but perfectly suits the couple who commissioned it.

The terrain is very steep, with spectacular views of the lake. The design adapts to the sloping terrain in an attempt to avoid large structures.

Local vernacular architecture inspired the design. Rain dominates the area, so sloped roofs suit both the terrain and the climate. The main construction materials were selected from the local industry and planned for easy maintenance: concrete and stone for the floors, fiberglass for the doors, and stucco walls.

The interior obtains a sense of "emptiness" by emphasizing the spaces rather than the decor. Art objects are placed at key places. The final effect is both elegant and informal.

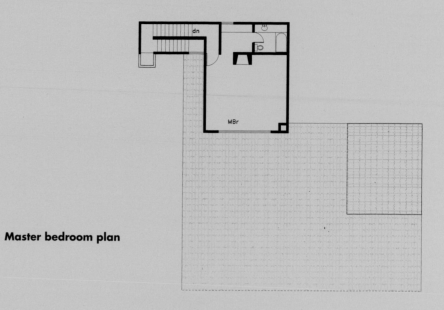

Master bedroom plan

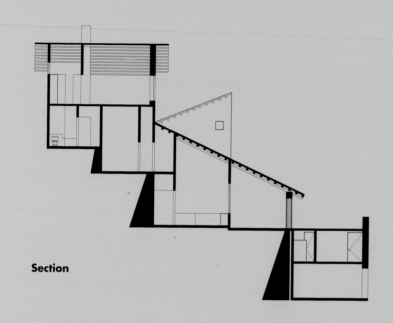

Section

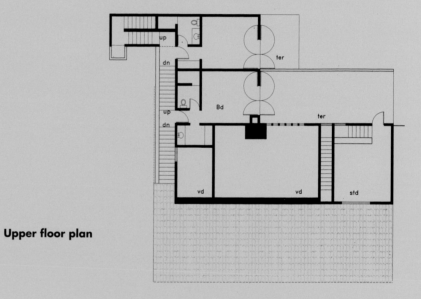

Upper floor plan

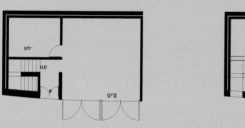

Entrance floor plan

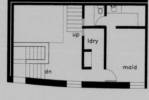

Service floor plan

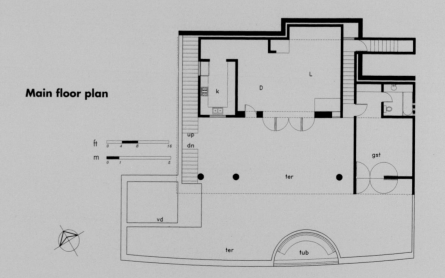

Main floor plan

Right: Bedroom courtyard

Opposite: Open-air living room

METROPOLITAN CATHEDRAL

Managua, Nicaragua, 1993

Images that remain permanently etched in one's memory are among life's most deeply touching experiences. The Metropolitan Cathedral in Nicaragua is one of these. Under the promotion and support of Cardinal Tom Monaghan, the cathedral became symbolic of the faith of a suffering country, the effort of the Nicaraguan Catholic people, the devotion of a cardinal, and hope for the people of Nicaragua.

In 1972 an earthquake destroyed Managua. The cathedral received extensive damage, making restoration infeasible. The new cathedral not only replaces the old but provides a new center for the capital.

The design recognizes that the role of the contemporary Catholic community has passed from passive to participatory in relation to the ecclesiastical authorities. The architectural integration of the altar and the assembly, and their physical proximity, follow this concept. For this reason the highest dome is located at the center of the congregation, not above the altar. This provides solemnity without resorting to monumentalism and ostentation while creating a scale in which worshipers will feel peaceful when alone, in small groups, or as part of a large congregation. The sixty-three domes evoke this range of scales and provide light and ventilation.

Three kinds of activities take place in the cathedral: several times a year the cardinal celebrates mass from the exterior altar above the main door to congregations of about 100,000 that gather in the esplanade; periodic ceremonies take place in this main space; and daily mass is celebrated in the chapel.

The venerated image of the Sangre de Cristo is located in a dedicated circular chapel. Its shape, illumination, candlelight, and color respond to Nicaraguan spiritual life. To provide protection against earthquakes, the walls are of reinforced concrete, chiseled by hand to represent the heroic strength of the people. The handmade cement tiles of the floor create a colored carpet of geometric forms. Colored screens emanate a special light throughout the interior, and the massive wood doors continue the imposing language of the exterior.

The cathedral's design and construction were driven by human and spiritual values, with the goal of offering the Nicaraguan people a place of hope, love, and prayer.

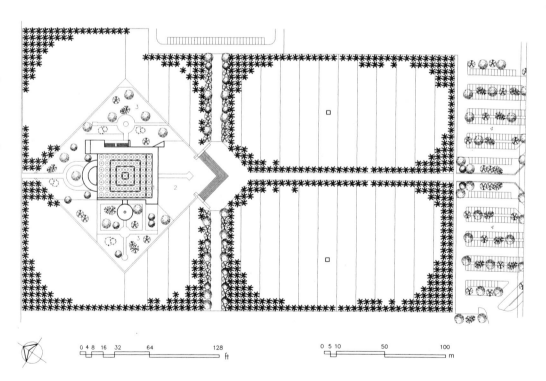

Site plan

1. Cathedral
2. Atrium
3. Garden
4. Parking

218

Left: The roof is a composition of 63 earthquake-resistant domes.

Opposite: A circular chapel dedicated to the image of the Sangre de Cristo was designed to respond to Nicaraguan spiritual life.

"A building is the result

of faith and effort . . .

the opportunity to contribute

to a country's renaissance

The unusual attitude

of a noble man,

together with a religious leader,

gave us the inspiration

to create a space

for prayer and meditation,

a unique experience

of humanism and belief. . .

the strongest

experience of my professional life."

R.L.

BIOGRAPHY OF RICARDO LEGORRETA

Education

1948–1952
Bachelor's degree in architecture,
Universidad Nacional Autónoma
de México

Professional Experience

1963–present
Principal of Legorreta Arquitectos, Mexico
City

1985–present
Founder and President of Legorreta
Arquitectos USA

1977
Founder and President of LA Designs,
a firm specializing in furniture and
accessories

1961–1963
Freelance activities

1955–1960
Partnership with architect José Villagrán
Garcia, Mexico

1948–1955
Draftsman and Project Manager for José
Villagrán Garcia, Mexico

Teaching Experience

Since 1969, Mr. Legorreta has lectured
throughout Mexico and in Canada,
Spain, Japan, Argentina, Chile,
Uruguay, Colombia, Guatemala, Costa
Rica, England, and Austria, and at more
than thirty universities in the United
States. He has been a professor at the
Universidad Nacional Autónoma de
México, Universidad Iberoamericana,
Harvard University, the University of
Texas at Austin, and the University of
California at Los Angeles.

Honors and Awards

1995
Design Award, First Kenneth F. Brown Asia
Pacific Culture and Architecture Design
Award Program of the MARCO
Contemporary Art Museum, Monterrey,
Mexico
Honor Award, AIA San Diego Chapter
(Chula Vista Library)

1994
AIA Award for Religious Architecture
(Metropolitan Cathedral, Managua)

1992
National Award of the Fine Arts
Architect of the Americas

1981–1994
Member of the Jury, The Pritzker Prize

1970–1981
Member, International Council, Museum of
Modern Art, New York

Honorary Fellow of the American Institute
of Architects
Member, International Academy of
Architecture
Member, Academy of Arts and Science,
Cambridge, Massachusetts
Advisor to the Chairman of the National
Council for the Arts and Culture, Mexico
Counselor for the Urban Development
Plan of Mexico City

LIST OF PROJECTS

Projects in bold are included in this volume.

1996–Present
Akle House
   Valle de Bravo, State of Mexico, Mexico
Alameda Project
   Mexico City
BANCEN
   Guadalajara, Jalisco, Mexico
Bilger House
   Los Angeles, California
Casa Jacinta and Víctor
   Mexico City
Cervantes House
   Mexico City
Cervantes House
   Valle de Bravo, State of Mexico, Mexico
Chiron Laboratories
   San Francisco, California
La Colorada House
   Valle de Bravo, State of Mexico, Mexico
Flynn House
   Miami, Florida
GBS Residential Learning Center
   Stanford University,
   Palo Alto, California
Medeiros House I
   Barra do Uma, Brazil
The Mexican Museum
   San Francisco, California
Ofer House
   Haifa, Israel
Tech Museum of Innovation
   San Jose, California
Televisa Headquarters
   Mexico City
International Student Center
   University of California at Los Angeles,
   Los Angeles, California
Visual Arts Center
   Santa Fe College,
   Santa Fe, New Mexico

1995
INVERLAT Office
   Mexico City
Hacienda Santana, residential complex
   Master plan and Club house
   State of Mexico, Mexico
Pasaje Santa Fe, housing
   Mexico City

San Antonio Main Library
San Antonio, Texas
Chula Vista Library
Chula Vista, California
Office Building
Monterrey, Nuevo León, Mexico

1994
City of the Arts
 Central Building and Administrative
 Tower, School of the Visual Arts,
 and Master Plan
 Mexico City
Monterrey Central Library
 Monterrey, Nuevo León, Mexico
Antigua Residential Complex
 Mexico City
Bankers Club
 Mexico City
Master Plan Santa Fe
 Mexico City
Pershing Square
 Los Angeles, California
Camino Real Mexico Hotel Remodel
 Mexico City
Chapultepec Zoo
 Mexico City
Garza Laguera House
 Monterrey, Nuevo León, Mexico

1993
El Papalote Children's Museum
 Mexico City
House in Sonoma
 Sonoma, California
Metropolitan Cathedral
 Managua, Nicaragua
Tech House
 Monterrey, Nuevo León, Mexico
Las Terrazas Office Building
 San Luis Potosí, San Luis Potosí, Mexico
Corporate Center Plaza Reforma
 Mexico City
Shapiro House
 Los Angeles, California
San Ildefonso Restoration
 Mexico City

1991
MARCO Contemporary Art Museum
 Monterrey, Nuevo León, Mexico
Greenberg House
 Los Angeles, California
Solana
 Village Center, IBM National Marketing
 and Technical Support Center
 Westlake-Southlake, Dallas, Texas
Conrad Cancún Hotel
 Cancún, Quintana Roo, México
Urban Design Guadalupe River Park
 San Jose, California

1989
Children's Discovery Museum
 San Jose, California
Marina Ground Facilities
 Cabo San Lucas, Baja California Sur,
 Mexico

1988
Banco Nacional de México Offices
 Mexico City
Zetune House
 Mexico City
Club Mediterranée
 Huatulco, Oaxaca, Mexico

1987
Rancho Santa Fe House
 Rancho Santa Fe, California
Banco Nacional de México Offices
 Tlalnepantla, State of Mexico, Mexico
Official Visitor's House FONATUR
 Huatulco, Oaxaca, Mexico

1985
Montalbán House
 Hollywood, California
Master Plan Huatulco
 Huatulco, Oaxaca, Mexico
Master Plan Westlake Park
 (in collaboration with Mitchell Giurgola,
 Barton Myers, and Peter Walker/
 Martha Schwartz)
 Westlake-Southlake, Dallas, Texas
Master Plan Valle de Bravo
 Valle de Bravo, State of Mexico, Mexico
Renault Factory
 Gómez Palacio, Durango, Mexico

1984
Cervantes House I
 Mexico City

1982
Urban Design Jurica City
 Querétaro, State of Querétaro, Mexico
Banco Nacional de México Offices
 Monterrey, Nuevo León, Mexico

1981
Camino Real Ixtapa Hotel
 Ixtapa, Guerrero, Mexico

1980
Lomas Sports Club
 Mexico City

1979
Beckmann House
 Valle de Bravo, State of Mexico, Mexico
Urban Design La Estadia
 State of Mexico, Mexico

1978
Las Brisas Hotel Remodel
 Acapulco, Guerrero, Mexico

1977
IBM Technical Center
 Mexico City

1976
Seguros Americana Office Building
 Mexico City
Gomez House II
 Mexico City
Low-Income Housing El Rosario
 INFONAVIT
 Mexico City

1975
Kodak Laboratories
 Mexico City
Camino Real Cancún Hotel
 Cancún, Quintana Roo, Mexico
IBM Factory
 Guadalajara, Jalisco, Mexico

1974
IBM Factory
 Mexico City

1973
Molinas House
 Mexico City
Gomez House I
 Mexico City
Valle House
 Valle de Bravo, State of Mexico, Mexico

1972
Palacio de Iturbide Restoration
 Mexico City
Office Building Insurgentes
 Mexico City
Hacienda Hotel
 Cabo San Lucas, Baja California Sur,
 Mexico

1970
Pedro de Gante School
 Tulancingo, Hidalgo, Mexico

1968
Celanese Mexicana, office building
 (in collaboration with Roberto Jean)
 Mexico City
Camino Real Mexico Hotel
 Mexico City
Plunket House
 Mexico City
Vallarta School
 Mexico City

1967
Cedros School
 Mexico City

1966
Nissan Mexicana Factory
 Cuernavaca, Morelos, Mexico
Legorreta Arquitectos Office
 Mexico City

1964
Smith Kline & French Laboratories
 Mexico City
Chrysler Factory
 Toluca, State of Mexico, Mexico

1963
Fabrica SF de Mexico
 Mexico City

SELECT BIBLIOGRAPHY

Books

Arquitectos Contemporáneos de México (Mexico City: Trillas, 1989), p. 94.

Attoe, Wayne. *The Architecture of Ricardo Legorreta* (Austin: The University of Texas Press, 1990).

Brown, E.; A. Petrina; H. Segawa; A. Toca; S. Trujillo. *Casas Latinoamericanas: Latin American Houses* (Barcelona: Editorial Gustavo Gili, 1994). FONATUR Huatulco House.

El Estudio del Arquitecto (Barcelona: Editorial Gustavo Gili, 1996).

IBM Westlake-Southlake (Denton Publishing Co., 1988). Solana.

Gabay y Bulbol, Pedro. *Ricardo Legorreta: Un Mexicano Arquitecto* (San Luis Potosí, Mexico: Pedro Gabay y Bulbol, 1988).

Martinez, Ernesto Alva. *La Casa en la Arquitectura Méxicana* (Mexico City: Comex, 1995), p. 118. Tech House Antigua.

———. *El Color en la Arquitectura Méxicana* (Mexico City: Comex, 1992), p. 38, 52, 86, 105, 107, 110, 113, 151, 183. Solana, Camino Real Mexico Hotel, Conrad Cancún Hotel, MARCO Contemporary Art Museum, Rancho Santa Fe House.

———. *Restauración y Remodelación en la Arquitectura* (Mexico City: Comex, 1994), p. 106. San Ildefonso Restoration.

Mereles, Louise Noelle. *Ricardo Legorreta: Tradición y Modernísmo* (Mexico City: Universidad Nacional Autónoma de México, 1989).

Zabalbeascoa, Anatxu. *La Casa del Arquitecto* (Barcelona: Editorial Gustavo Gili, 1995). Valle House.

———. *The House of the Architect* (New York: Rizzoli International Publications, 1995). Valle House.

Articles

Unless otherwise noted, magazines and journals listed below with Spanish titles were published in Mexico.

1996

"La Cattedrale di Managua," *Abitare*, January 1996.

"Museo de Arte Contemporaneo," *Arquitectura Panamericana*, April 1996, p. 18.

"National Center of the Arts," *Architectural Record*, March 1996.

"Special Model," *Madame Figaro*, March 1996.

"Tec Museum, Biblioteca Sn. Antonio, Biblioteca Monterrey," *Arquitectura*, January 1996.

1995

"Arquitecturas do Mundo, E Viva o México!" *Arquitectura & Construção* (Brazil), March 1995, p. 12.

"Enchilada Red Easy Winner as Color for New S. A. Library," *San Antonio Express News*, February 12, 1995, p. 1B.

"Greenberg House," *Buzz: The Talk of Los Angeles,* May 1995, p. 103.

"Imagenes Centro Nacional de las Artes," *Entorno Inmobiliario*, January-February 1995, p. 40. City of the Arts.

"It's Legorreta," *Progressive Architecture*, June 1995, p. 53. San Antonio Library.

"Laviada House," *GA Houses Project 45*, March 1995, p. 124. La Colorada House.

"Rebuilding Mexico City Part II: Through Architecture," *Insite Podio* (Canada), January 1995, p. 52. City of the Arts.

"Ricardo Legorreta Addresses AIA Regional Conference," *Designer Builder*, November 1995, p. 25.

"Ricardo Legorreta: Chiron Corporation Life Sciences Center," *GA Document International 43*, September 1995, p. 2.

"The East-West Encounter," *Hawaii Pacific Architecture*, August 1995, p. 32. MARCO Contemporary Art Museum.

"Un Oasis de Colores," *El Cronista Arquitecto*, April 12, 1995. Chula Vista Library.

"Word from the West," *Interior Design*, February 1995, p. 32. MARCO Contemporary Art Museum.

Arnoboldi, Mario Antonio. "Il Dominio e l'Ambiente," *L'Arca* (Italy), January 1995, p. 48. Greenberg House.

Dillon, David. "San Antonio Library," *Architecture*, October 1995, p. 80.

Donegan, Craig. "San Antonio's New Library," *San Antonio Express News*, May 14, 1995, p. 21.

Fontana, Jacopo della. "Nella Sfera del Colore, Mexican Colours," *L'Arca* (Italy), May 1995, p. 54. El Papalote Children's Museum.

Glusberg, Jorge. "Un Arquitecto Mexicano Universal," *CP 67 News* (Argentina), January 1995, p. 2. Club Med Huatulco Hotel, Renault Factory, Solana, Montalbán House, Tech House, IBM Technical Center Mexico, Rancho Santa Fe House, Camino Real Ixtapa Hotel.

Ingersoll, Richard. "Del Rosa al Amarillo," *Arquitectura Viva* (Spain), January-February 1995, p. 20. Legorreta Arquitectos Office, Renault Factory, Chrysler Factory, MARCO Contemporary Art Museum, Camino Real Mexico Hotel, El Papalote Children's Museum, Chapultepec Zoo, Shapiro House.

Jarmusch, Ann. "Libraries for the 21st Century," *San Diego Union Tribune*, June 3, 1995, p. A18.

Marquez, Francesca Garcia. "Il Volume del Colore," *L'Arca* (Italy), March 1995, p. 62. MARCO Contemporary Art Museum.

Monge, Raul. "Continua el Plan del Alameda," *Proceso*, July 1995, p. 68.

Russell, Jan. "Seeing Red," *Texas Monthly*, November 1995, p. 112. San Antonio Main Library.

Webb, Michael. "El Idioma del Color: Luis Barragán y Ricardo Legorreta," *Diseño Interior 39* (Spain), 1995, p. 8. Legorreta Arquitectos Office, Greenberg House, Rancho Santa Fe House, Gomez House I, Solana, San Jose Children's Museum, Pershing Square, Camino Real Mexico Hotel, Gomez House II.

Whiteson, Leon. "Legorreta on Legorreta," *Elle Decor*, February-March 1995, p. 129.

1994

"Arquitecto Victor," *Insite Podio* (Canada), July 1994, p. 8. Greenberg House, Metropolitan Cathedral, El Papalote Children's Museum.

"La Arquitectura del Conservatorio y las Escuelas de Teatro y Danza," *Proceso*, November 1994, p. 60. City of the Arts.

"Cathedral de Managua," *a+u*, October 1994, p. 8. Metropolitan Cathedral, Pershing Square.

"Edificio Central y Torre de Investigaciones del CNA," *Arquitectura*, 1994, p. 50. City of the Arts.

"En el Limite de la Arquitectura y la Escultura," *Contactos Fomento Cultural Banamex*, 1994, p. 32. Camino Real Ixtapa Hotel, Metropolitan Cathedral.

"House in Northern California," *GA Houses 42*, June 1994, p. 40. House in Sonoma.

"Legorreta Constructor de Catedrales," *Arquitectura Viva* (Spain), July-August 1994.

"Painting Pershing Purple," *Progressive Architecture*, September 1994.

"Pershing Returns," *Los Angeles Downtown News*, January 31, 1994.

"Plain Air and Simple," *Los Angeles Times Magazine*, September 1994.

"San Jose Tech Museum Expansion Set," *San Francisco Chronicle*, June 28, 1994, p. A13.

"Templo para la Fé Nicaraguense," *Projecto*, April 1994. Metropolitan Cathedral.

Argueta, Fernando. "El proyecto cultural mas ambicioso de esta administración: La Ciudad de las Artes," *Epoca*, March 1994, p. 68. City of the Arts.

Branch, Mark Alden. "Silence at Solana," *Progressive Architecture*, December 1994, p. 74.

Espetia, Gustavo. "Aprendo Jugando," *Arquitectura*, May 1994, p. 70. El Papalote Children's Museum.

Fernandez, Antonio Toca. "La Fuerza de la Esperanza," *A&V 48* (Spain), 1994, p. 86. Metropolitan Cathedral.

Filla, Martin. "Open House," *Town and Country*, December 1994, p. 170. House in Sonoma.

Glusberg, Jorge. "Misterio y Conciencia en la Obra de Ricardo Legorreta," *Revista El Arquitecto de Córdoba*, November 1994, p. 29. Camino Real Cancún Hotel, Montalbán House, Solana, Camino Real Mexico Hotel.

Gordon, Larry. "A Push to Take Back the Parks," *Los Angeles Times*, January 29, 1994. Pershing Square.

Gregory, Daniel. "Downtown Reborn," *Sunset*, May 1994, p. 86. Pershing Square.

Grunhut, Silvia. "Purisima Concepción," *Cordialidad Volumen 6* (Panama), 1994–1995, p. 14. Metropolitan Cathedral.

Macedo, Luis Ortiz. "Camino Real México: Un Hotel un Museo," "Arquitectura Mexicana Reflexiones," *Artes de México*, Spring 1994, p. 129. Camino Real Mexico Hotel, Camino Real Ixtapa Hotel.

Marquez, Francesca Garcia. "Il Projetto del Vuoto," *L'Arca* (Italy), May 1994, p. 40. Pershing Square.

Mereles, Louise Noelle. "Un Estilo de Vida Diferente," *Entorno Inmobiliario*, September-October 1994, p. 28. Pasaje Santa Fe.

Rivera, Hector. *Proceso*, October 1994, p. 58. Metropolitan Cathedral, Chapultepec Zoo, El Papalote Children's Museum, City of the Arts.

Rodriguez, Ignacio. "Un clasico contemporaneo que vuelve a sus origenes," *Vacaciones*, July 1994, p. 68. Camino Real Mexico Hotel.

Sherr, Leslie H. "The Architecture of Emotion," *Graphics* 295, January-February 1994, p. 2. Conrad Cancún Hotel, Solana, Legorreta Arquitectos Office.

Stein, Karen. "Where the Streets Have No Name," *Architectural Record*, July 1994, p. 70. Metropolitan Cathedral.

Varela, Orlando. "MARCO, Espacio para la Cultura en el Norte de México," *Diversión*, August 1994, p. 64.

Webb, Michael. "Common Ground," *db: Deutsche Bauzeitung* (Germany), June 1994, p. 140.

1993

"Caminos Realidades," *Colaboradores Camino Real México*, September 1993. Camino Real Mexico Hotel.

"Job of a Lifetime: The Design of Israel's Supreme Court," *Progressive Architecture*, April 1993.

"La Poética del Angulo Recto," *A&V* 9 (Spain), January-February 1993, p. 104. MARCO Contemporary Art Museum.

"LA's Playa Vista Plan Approved by City," *Progressive Architecture*, November 1993.

"Legorreta y sus Museos," *Enlace*, November 1993, p. 60. San Ildefonso Restoration, El Papalote Children's Museum.

"México Color y Aqua," *Arquitectura El Nacional*, September 22, 1993. Camino Real Ixtapa Hotel.

"Museo del Niño," *ICA 85*, May-June 1993, p. 14. El Papalote Children's Museum.

"Museu MARCO," *Arquitectura Urbanismo* (Brazil), June-July l993, p. 28.

"Ricardo Legorreta," *GA Document* 36, May 1993, p. 54. El Papalote Children's Museum.

"Ricardo Legorreta," *Nikkei Architecture* 3:1 (1993), p. 173. Legorreta Arquitectos Office.

GA Houses 39, November 1993, p. 102. Shapiro House.

Glusberg, Jorge. "Un Museo en Monterrey," *Projeto* (Brazil), August 1993, p. 80. MARCO Contemporary Art Museum.

———. "Una Casa Mexicana para el Museo de Arte de Monterrey," *Personas* 4 (Argentina), 1993, p. 54. MARCO Contemporary Art Museum.

Hollenstein, Roman. "Ein Hauch Von Mexiko," *Nzz Folio* (Germany), March 1993, p. 64. Greenberg House.

Mereles, Louise Noelle. "Regionalism and the Vanguard," *World Architecture*, January 1993, p. 48. Renault Factory, San Jose Children's Museum, Solana, Kodak Laboratories, MARCO Contemporary Art Museum.

Millares, E. "Locura Cromatica," *La Casa de Marie Claire*, June 1993, p. 68. Cervantes House.

Rigo, Jose. "Libros: La Arquitectura de Ricardo Legorreta," *Arquitectura*, January 1993, p. 72.

Rivera, Hector. "Repaso Critico a la Arquitectura Mexicana del Siglo," *Proceso*, March 1993, p. 44.

Sarzabal, Hernan Barbero. "México Color y Aqua," *Arquitecto y Diseño* (Argentina), March 31, 1993. Camino Real Ixtapa Hotel.

Sollins, Dena. "Mexico Market Heats Up for Us Architects," *The American Institute of Architects Memo*, September 1993, p. 15. Urban Design La Estadia.

Vivar, Rodrigo. "Espacios Culturales de la Postmodernidad," *Escala*, October 1993, p. 90. MARCO Contemporary Art Museum.

1992

"Architettura e Spazio Sacro Nella Modernità," *Abitare Segesta Spa* (Italy), December 1992, p. 278. Metropolitan Cathedral.

"Estilo Humor y Arquitectura," *Obras*, December 1992, Solana, Molina House, Gomez House II, Chrysler Factory.

"Market Forces," *The Architectural Review*, September 1992, p. 68. Tustin Market.

"Ricardo Legorreta Vilchis," *Lideres Mexicanos*, June 1992, p. 81.

"San Ildefonso Restauración y Deterioro," *Excelsior News*, August 23, 1992, p. 4.

"The Wall in México," *a+u*, October 1992, p. 58. Legorreta Arquitectos Office, Renault Factory, Solana, Metropolitan Cathedral, FONATUR Huatulco House, San Jose Children's Museum, Conrad Cancún Hotel, MARCO Contemporary Art Museum.

Bolivier, M. "La Restauración del Colegio de San Ildefonso," *Excelsior News*, August 18, 1992.

Borghi, Ruagero. "L'Oasi Segreta," *Ville Giardini*, June 1992, p. 4. Greenberg House.

Bustamante, Veronica Maza. "Misteriosa Remodelación," *Ovaciones News*, August 18, 1992. San Ildefonso Restoration.

Fernandez, Antonio Toca. "A Casa—Refugio," *Arquitectura Urbanismo* 40 (Brazil), 1992, p. 62. Greenberg House, Camino Real Cancún Hotel, Solana, IBM Technical Center Mexico, Camino Real Mexico Hotel.

Ferrer, Martin Luis Guzman. "San Ildefonso Restoration," *El Excelsior News*, December 1, 1992, p. 7A.

Gonzalez, Tomas. "La Casa Mixteca," *Kena*, January 1992, p. 30. FONATUR Huatulco House.

Goya, Manuel. "En la Frontera," *Casa Vogue España*, June 1992, p. 132. Montalbán House.

Mereles, Louise Noelle. "Legorreta Regionalismo e Vanguarda," *Projeto* (Brazil), March 1992, p. 29. Solana, Legorreta Arquitectos Office, Camino Real Mexico Hotel, Camino Real Cancún Hotel, Financial Center Monterrey, IBM Technical Center Mexico, Renault Factory, Camino Real Ixtapa Hotel, FONATUR Huatulco House.

———. "San Ildefonso Restoration," *Novedades News*, December 11, 1992, p. C17.

———. "Tre Architetti Messicani," "Museo delle Scaperele per i Bambini," *L'Architettura*, July-August 1992, p. 518. San Jose Children's Museum.

Steel, James. "Ricardo Legorreta," "Architecture in Development," *Mimar* 43, Spring 1992, p. 62. Chrysler Factory, Metropolitan Cathedral, Renault Factory, Camino Real Ixtapa Hotel, Solana, Conrad Cancún Hotel.

Stein, Karen D. "Greenberg House." *GA Houses* 33, February 1992, p. 10. Greenberg House.

Velazquez, Gloria. "Destruyen el Colegio San Ildefonso," *Excelsior News*, August 30, 1992, p. 5.

Viladas, Pilar. "The Poetry of Walls," *House and Garden*, February 1992, p. 116. Greenberg House.

1991

"Architecture of Light," *Annual Luce* (Italy), 1991, p. 32. Renault Factory, Solana, Camino Real Ixtapa Hotel.

"Arquitectos de México," *Geomundo*, August 1991, p. 164. Camino Real Cancún Hotel, Camino Real Ixtapa Hotel, IBM Factory Guadalajara.

"Creating Common Ground," *Los Angeles Times*, August 11, 1991. Pershing Square.

"Design Approach: Ricardo Legorreta," *AD 100 Architects*, August 1991, p. 148. Montalbán House.

"Un Espacio Para la Cultura Contemporánea," *Suplemento Especial del Norte*, June 28, 1991. MARCO Contemporary Art Museum.

"Legorreta Team Wins San Antonio Library," *Progressive Architecture*, September 1991, p. 24.

"Museo de Arte Contemporaneo," *Casas y Gente*, November 1991.

"Para México y el Mundo," *Monterrey Review*, Summer 1991, p. 22. MARCO Contemporary Art Museum.

"A Remarkable Place in the Sun," *Southern Accents*, February 1991, p. 28. Solana.

"Ricardo Legorreta," *Architectural Digest*, AD 100 Architects, July 1991.

"Ricardo Legorreta: Metropolitan Cathedral Managua, Nicaragua," *GA Document International* 29, April 1991, p. 58.

"Ricardo Legorreta: Vision for Our New Library," *San Antonio Light*, July 14, 1991, p. A2.

"Secret Garden/Greenberg House," *Architectural Record Houses*, December 1991.

"Someday in the Park," *Los Angeles Downtown News*, May 27, 1991. Pershing Square.

"Tradición y Modernidad,"*Arquitectura Viva* (Spain), January-February 1991, p. 47.

Carbonell, Dolores. "Una Charla con Ricardo Legorreta," *Linaje*, December 1991, p. 115. Camino Real Mexico Hotel.

Crosbie, Michael J. "Child's Play," *Architecture*, September 1991, p. 59. San Jose Children's Museum.

Dermansky, Ann. "The Most Astounding Pools in the World," *Elle Decor*, August 1991, p. 37, 42, 46, 94, 95. Camino Real Ixtapa Hotel, Cerisola House, Valle House II, Palacio de Versalles House, Club Med Huatulco Hotel.

Greenberg, Mike. "Reading the Library," *San Antonio Express News* (Texas), September 1, 1991, p. 1H.

Herkenhoff, Paulo. "Global Outreach Latin America," *Art News*, October 1991, p. 88. MARCO Contemporary Art Museum.

Jimenez, Carlos. "El Hotel en la Pradera," *Arquitectura Viva* (Spain), November-December 1991, p. 40. Solana Marriott Hotel.

Kalach, Alberto. "Museo del Niño: Tres Propuestas," *Arquitectura* 1 (1991), p. 14. El Papalote Children's Museum.

Murtinho, Pedro. "La Arquitectura Como Vida," *Diseño* 9 (Chile), September-October 1991, p. 60. Camino Real Mexico Hotel, Financial Center Monterrey, Conrad Cancún Hotel, Seguros America Offices, Renault Factory, Solana, Legorreta Arquitectos Office, El Rosario, Club Med Huatulco hotel, Montalbán House, La Estadia, Gomez House I.

Rosas, Leo. "Un Marco Perfecto para la Plastica," *Casas y Gente*, November 1991, p. 13. MARCO Contemporary Art Museum.

Tilley, Don. "Legorreta Project Bridges Two Countries," *Architecture NY*, September 1991, p. 22. MARCO Contemporary Art Museum.

Viladas, Pilar. "Secret Garden," *Architectural Record Houses*, April 1991, p. 116. Greenberg House.

1990

"Beyond Barragan: Mexican Architecture Today," *Architectural Record*, May 1990, p. 59. Renault Factory.

"Solana Business Park in Texas," *Baumeister* (Germany), April 1990, p. 32.

Anella, Tony. "Solana: A Place in the Sun," *Artpace* (Albuquerque), June 1990.

Browne, Enrique, and Mariana Novoa. "Espacios de Legorreta," *Ladeco America* (Chile), May 1990, p. 80. Financial Center Monterrey, Legorreta Arquitectos Office, Camino Real Ixtapa Hotel.

Cantu, Donald J. "At Home in San Jose," *Architectural Record*, September 1990. San Jose Children's Museum.

Dillon, David. "And Two in the Country," *Landscape Architecture*, March 1990, p. 62. Solana.

———. "Of the Land," *Architecture*, November 1990, p. 94. Solana.

Mereles, Louise Noelle. "South of the Border," *Blueprint*, April 1990, p. 56. Renault Factory.

———. "The Hues of Solace," *World Architecture* 5 (1990), p. 54. IBM Factory Guadalajara, Renault Factory, Financial Center Monterrey, Legorreta Arquitectos Office.

1989

"Hotel Camino Real Ixtapa," *Ars*, July 1989, p. 100.

"IBM Westlake-Southlake," *Process* (Tokyo), October 1989, p. 106. Solana.

"Legorreta Arquitectos IBM Southlake and Village Center Solana West-Southlake," *GA Document* 23, April 1989, p. 20.

"Legorreta Arquitectos IBM Southlake and Village Center Solana. Westlake-Southlake Texas, 1986–1989," *GA Document* 24, August 1989.

"Meet the Architect," *GA Houses*, March 1989, p. 32. Valle House, Molina House, Gomez House I and II, Cervantes House, Montalbán House, Rancho Santa Fe House, Zetune House.

"A Place in the Sun," *Identity*, Fall 1989, p. 53, Solana.

"Super Teamwork Forges 'Age-Proof' IBM Center," *Facilities Design & Management*, February 1989. IBM Technical Center Mexico.

Aldunate, Ana Francisca, and Manena Fabres. "Esto es Ixtapa," *Ladeco America* (Chile), November-December 1989, p. 76. Camino Real Ixtapa Hotel.

Barna, Joel W. "Solana in the Sun," *Progressive Architecture*, April 1989, p. 45.

Dillon, David. "IBM's Colorful Place in the Sun," *Architecture*, May 1989, p. 100. Solana.

Gardino, Alberto. "Il Profeta dello Stile Mexico," *La Mia Casa*, November 1989, p. 56. Rancho Santa Fe House.

Goldberger, Paul. "IBM's Urbane New Place in the Sun in Texas," *The New York Times*, October 1989, p. 42. Solana.

Laurence, John F. "Nice Profits from Better City," *Fortune*, October 1989, p. 74. Solana.

Mereles, Louise Noelle. "Ricardo Legorreta Tradición y Modernidad," *Colección de Artes* 41 Universidad Nacional Autónoma de México (1989), Camino Real Ixtapa Hotel, Financial Center Monterrey, Renault Factory, Montalbán House, Urban Design La Estadia, El Rosario, Solana, Pedro de Gante School, Cabo San Lucas Hotel, Valle House, Gomez House I, IBM Factory Guadalajara, Camino Real Cancún Hotel, IBM Technical Center Mexico.

———. *Arquitectos Contemporáneos de México Trillas*, 1989, p. 94.

Pani, Mario. "Regionalismo Universal: Bienvenido al Arquitecto Ricardo Legorreta en su Ingreso a la Academia de Artes," *México en el Arte*, April 1989, p. 23. Solana, Rancho Santa Fe House, Montalbán House.

Posner, Ellen. "Architecture: Visiting Solana," *The Wall Street Journal*, November 8, 1989.

University of California at San Diego. "Ricardo Legorreta: True Values of Architecture," *Architecture/Shaping the Future*, February 1989, p. 5. Renault Factory, Camino Real Ixtapa Hotel, Solana, Rancho Santa Fe House.

1988

"IBM Westlake-Southlake: Hot Colors and Cool Woods Make IBM Venture a Surprise," *Fort Worth Star Telegram*, November 16, 1988, p. 3. Solana.

"Painting the Prairie: IBM Westlake-Southlake," *The Dallas Morning News*, October 9, 1988, sec. C. Solana.

Bruche, Sam. "Echoes of México: Ricardo Montalban's House Represents a Fusion of Cultures," *Los Angeles Times Magazine*, June 28, 1988, p. 27.

Marti, Beatriz, and Kateri Aragon. "Ciudades Turísticas, Una Estrategia Mexicana de Desarrollo," *Fondo Nacional de Fomento al Turísmo*, November 15, 1988, p. 42, 77, 168. Camino Real Cancún Hotel, Camino Real Ixtapa Hotel, Club Med Huatulco hotel.

Putnam, Judy. "Computer Age Enters Westlake," *Fort Worth Star Telegram*, July 3, 1988. Solana.

1987

"Renault Ricardo Legorreta," *Center*, Center for the Study of American Architecture, School of Architecture, University of Texas at Austin, 1987, p. 82, 126.

Budd, Jim, and Luis Ortiz Macedo. "Una Tradición de Camino Real," *Excelencia*, Fall 1987, p. 21, 55. Camino Real Mexico Hotel.

El Viajero, Juan. "Juan Viajero," *Excelencia*, Summer 1987, p. 78. Jurica Urban Design.

Fuentes, Carlos. "The Los Angeles Residence of Georgiana and Ricardo Montalban," *Architectural Digest*, March 1987, p. 166, 171.

1986

"Mexico's Quiet Pacific Playground," *The New York Times*, February 16, 1986, Camino Real Ixtapa Hotel.

Caloca. "Camino Real Ixtapa," *Excelencia*, Fall 1986, p. 57.

Osorio, Nicolas Sanchez. "El Patio del Sol," *Casas y Gente*, June 1986, p. 21, Camino Real Ixtapa Hotel.

1985

"A Style for the Year 2001: What is the Future of Architecture," *Zigurat Shinkenchiku*, Summer 1985, p. 140.

"The Wall in Mexico: Ricardo Legorreta," *Archidemia*, Fall 1985.

Osorio, Nicolas Sanchez. "Palacio de Iturbide y Suite Camino Real México," *Casas y Gente*, December 1985, p. 58.

Warfield, James P. "Legorreta and the Wall Culture: a Case Study in Architecture Nationalism," *UIA: XV Congreso Mundial de la Union Internacional de Arquitectos* (Cairo), January 1985.

1984

"Hotel Camino Real Ixtapa," *a+u*, September 1984, p. 57.

"A New Playground for the Pacific," *Signature*, January 1984. Camino Real Ixtapa Hotel.

Fuentes, Carlos. "Mexico's Two Seas," *The New York Times Magazine*, March 1984, p. 34. Camino Real Ixtapa Hotel.

1983

"An Architect's Grand Gesture on a Low Budget," *Los Angeles Times Home*, November 13, 1983, p. 14. Valle House II.

"Camino Real Ixtapa, Terraced Seas the Hotel," *Architecture*, August 1983, p. 178.

"Evolution of the Red," *a+u*, September 1983.

"Hotel Camino Real Ixtapa," *The AIA Journal*, August 1983.

"Ricardo Legorreta," *CA 35: IV Bienal de Arquitectura* (Chile), August 1983, p. 118. Camino Real Ixtapa Hotel.

"Ricardo Legorreta," *NasDom* (Yugoslavia), February 1983, p. 33. Camino Real Mexico Hotel, Camino Real Ixtapa Hotel, Valle House, Gomez House I.

"Ricardo Legorreta," *Process*, November 1983.

"Simplificación Llevada al Minimo," *Obras*, January 1983, p. 30. IBM Factory Guadalajara.

"Telas Ligeras," *Vogue*, April 1983. Camino Real Ixtapa Hotel.

David, Theoharis. "Search for Identity," *Architecture*, October 1983, p. 24. Pedro de Gante School, Gomez House I.

1957–1982

"Architects: Ricardo Legorreta," *a+u*, September-October 1978, p. 115–120. Valle House.

"Camino Real Cancun Hotel," *Landscape Architecture*, November 1977.

"Casa Habitación en una Barranca," *Arquitectos de México*, December 1962.

"Casa Habitación, Valle de Bravo," *Arquitectura/Mexico*, September-October 1978. Valle House.

"Casa en Valle de Bravo, Mexico," *Suma*, July 1979. Valle House.

"Celanese Mexicana," *The New Magazine*, October 1967.

"A Concern for Form and Space," *Los Angeles Times Home*, June 1973.

"Con El Sello de Un Estilo," *Obras*, April 1978, p. 20. Banamex Office Building.

"Discover Mexico," *Vogue*, September 1977.

"¿Dónde trabajas? Fabrica Automex en Toluca" *Calli*, February 1964, p. 17. Chrysler Factory.

"Dos Edificios Ejemplares," *El Nacional*, February 1976.

"Edificio de Celanese Mexicana," *En Concreto*, September-October 1968.

"Edificio de Oficinas Para Celanese," *Arquitectura México*, April 1970. Celanese Mexicana.

"El Almacen del Siglo XX," *Obras*, May 1979, p. 23. IBM Factory Guadalajara.

"Entrevista al Arq. Legorreta y al Arq. Castro," *Arquitectos de México*, August 1967, p. 28. Camino Real Mexico Hotel, Nissan Factory, Chrysler Factory, John Deere Factory, Smith Klein & French Laboratories, Vallarta School, Cedros School, Legorreta Arquitectos Office.

"Everyman's Mexican Home," *Progressive Architecture*, June 1969.

"Fabrica en Tlanepantla," *Arquitectos de México*, June 1962.

"Hotel Camino Real Mexico," *Arquitectura México*, November 1969.

"Hotel Camino Real Mexico," *The Architectural Forum*, November 1968.

"La Plaza de los Conos," *Progressive Architecture*, June 1966, p. 20. Chrysler Factory.

"La Relación Arquitecto-Ingeniero," *Instituto Mexicano del Cemento y del Concreto*, May-June 1972.

"The Many Faces of Mexico," *Los Angeles Times Home*, June 17, 1973, p. 18. Molina House.

"Mexico Today, A New City," *Los Angeles Times Home*, February 1976.

"Modern Living: Camino Real Mexico Hotel," *Time*, October 11, 1968, p. 61.

"A Palacio of Commerce," *Architecture Plus*, June 1973.

"Palacio de Iturbide," *Constru-Noticias*, June 1973.

"Palacio de Iturbide," *Design*, July 1957.

"Planta IBM Guadalajara, Mexico," *Arquitectura México*, July/August, 1977.

"Planta IBM Guadalajara, Mexico," *Obras*, July 1977.

"Resort Condominium in Mexico," *Baumeister* (Germany), May 1977.

"Ricardo Legorreta," *Arquitectura México*, April-July 1968, p. 30. Fabrica SF de Mexico, John Deere Factory, Legorreta Arquitectos Office, Camino Real Ciudad Juarez Hotel, Trmec Factory, Nissan Factory, El Molino Ranch, Vallarta School, Celanese Mexicana, Chrysler Factory.

"Ricardo Legorreta," *GA Houses*, May 14, 1981, p. 54. Gomez House I.

"Ricardo Legorreta: El Arquitecto Mexicano de México," *Enfoques Mexicanos Sumarios* 39 (January 1980). Chrysler Factory, Fabrica SF de Mexico, Valle House, El Rosario, Camino Real Cancún Hotel, Camino Real Mexico Hotel, Camino Real Cabo San Lucas Hotel, IBM Factory Guadalajara.

"Una Planta con Dimensión Humana," *Obras*, February 1976, p. 12. IBM Factory Guadalajara.

"Walls: a Special and Functional Drama," *Los Angeles Times Home*, November 1981.

Atman, Gloria. "Hacer una Arquitectura Congruente con el País," *Razones*, May 1982, p. 55. IBM Technical Center Mexico.

Attoe, Wayne. "Thick, Rough, Malleable," *Progressive Architecture*, September 1980, p. 184. IBM Technical Center Mexico, Camino Real Cancún Hotel.

Campillo, Bona. "Moda Ixtapeña," *Claudia*, September 1982, p. 42. Camino Real Ixtapa Hotel.

Clark, Kenneth N., and Patricia Daylone. "Desert Housing in Baja California." In *Desert Housing*, 1980, p. 237. Camino Real Cabo San Lucas Hotel.

Diaz de Ovando, Clementina. "El Palacio de Iturbide," *Artes de México* 179–180 (1977), p. 134.

Legorreta, Ricardo. "Los Complejos Sociales y Disneylandia," *Arquitectura México*, November-December 1976, p. 107.

———. "Muros de México," *San Angel Ediciones*, November 10, 1978.

———. "Un Experimento de Crítica Arquitectonica," *Arquitectura México*, January 1967, p. 165. Vallarta School.

MacMasters, Dan. "Consistency and Change," *Los Angeles Times Home*, May 14, 1978, p. 10. Gomez House I.

———. "Mexico Today: Valle II," *Los Angeles Times*, February 15, 1976, p. 12.

———. "The Dunes of Cabo San Lucas," *Los Angeles Times Home*, May 1974, p. 68.

———. "The Language of Color," *Los Angeles Times Home*, October 28, 1979, p. 17. IBM Technical Center Mexico.

Patronato Cultural del Instituto del Fondo Nacional de la Vivienda Para los Trabajadores. "Unidad Habitacional El Rosario," *La Ciudad en La Ciudad*, 1976, p. C1.

Rodes, Barbara. "Hotel Camino Real Mexico," *Moebel Interior Design* (Germany), October 1969, p. 41.

Smith, C. Ray. "Low Density in the Dunes," *Progressive Architecture*, September 1976, p. 68. Camino Real Cabo San Lucas Hotel.

———. "The Mexican Minimalism of Ricardo Legorreta," *Architectural Record*, October 1976, p. 97. IBM Factory Guadalajara, Camino Real Cancún Hotel.

Southern California Institute of Architecture. "Ricardo Legorreta," *Modern Architecture: Mexico*, May-June 1981, p. 36.

PROJECT CREDITS

Legorreta Arquitectos Office

Client: Legorreta Arquitectos
Size: 5,500 sq. ft.
Architectural Design and Landscape
 Architecture: Ricardo Legorreta, Noé
 Castro, Carlos Vargas
Structural Design: Bernardo Calderón,
 José Luis Calderón

Camino Real Mexico Hotel

Client: Banco Nacional de México,
 Westin International Hotels
Size: 900,000 sq. ft.
Architectural Design and Landscape
 Architecture: Ricardo Legorreta,
 Carlos Hernández, Ramiro Alatorre,
 Noé Castro
Structural Design: Bernardo Calderón,
 José Luis Calderón
Hydraulic Design: Ingeniería
 Panamericana, S. A.
Structural Consultant: Dr. Leonardo
 Zeevaert
Interior Design: Knoll Internacional, S. A.
Graphic Design: Lance Wyman

MARCO Contemporary Art Museum

Client: Patronato Museo de Arte
 Contemporáneo
Size: 215,000 sq. ft.
Architectural Design, Interiors and
 Landscape Architecture: Ricardo
 Legorreta, Víctor Legorreta, Noé Castro
Design Team: Carlos Villela, Erica Krayer,
 Joaquin Pineda
Structural Design:Raúl Izquierdo
HVAC: Calefacción y Ventilación,
 S. A. de C. V.
Hydraulic and Electrical Design:
 ITECNIE y Asociados, S. A.
Lighting Design: Fisher Marantz Reufro
 Stone
Contractor: Rafael Garza
Graphic Design: Lance Wyman

El Papalote Children's Museum

Client: Fundación Museo de Niños
Size: 6,000 sq. ft.
Architectural Design and Landscape
 Architecture: Ricardo Legorreta, Víctor
 Legorreta, Noé Castro
Design Team: Francisco Vivas, Juan Carlos
 Nolasco, Alejandro Betancourt,
 Guillermo Díaz de Sandi
Structural Design: Raúl Izquierdo
Mechanical and Electrical Design: Hubard
 y Bourlon
Contractor: ICA Construcción Urbana

Cervantes House

Client: Mr. and Mrs. Luis Cervantes
Size: 7,000 sq. ft.
Architectural Design: Ricardo Legorreta,
 Víctor Legorreta, Noé Castro
Associate Architect: Chávez Vigil
 Arquitectos
Structural Design: Ricardo Camacho
Mechanical Design: DIIN/Alejandro
 Borboa
Contractor: Armando Chávez/José Vigil

Camino Real Ixtapa Hotel

Client: Banco Nacional de México, Westin
 International Hotels
Size: 490,000 sq. ft.
Architectural Design, Interiors and
 Landscape Architecture: Ricardo
 Legorreta, Noé Castro, Carlos Vargas
Design Team: Gerardo Alonso
Structural and Mechanical Design:
 DIRAC, S. A. de C. V.
Electrical Design: BIPSA
Contractor: Gutsa, ECSA, Bolaños, Los
 Remedios

Renault Factory

Client: Renault Industrias Mexicanas,
 S. A. de C. V.
Size: 800,000 sq. ft.
Architectural Design and Landscape
 Architecture: Ricardo Legorreta, Noé
 Castro
Design Team: Gerardo Alonso
Structural, Mechanical, Electrical Design:
 AINSA Ingenieros, S. A. de C. V.
Awards: Silver Medal, First Mexican
 Architecture Biennial, 1990

Tech House

Client: Instituto Tecnológico de Enseñanza
 e Investigación Superior (ITESM)
Size: 19,000 sq. ft.
Architectural Design, Interiors and
 Landscape Architecture: Ricardo
 Legorreta, Víctor Legorreta, Noé Castro
Design Team: Héctor Cavazos, Erica
 Krayer, Alice Longoria
Interior Design: Legorreta Arquitectos/
 Erica Krayer, Alice Longoria
Structural, Mechanical, Electrical Design:
 ITESM Monterrey
Contractor: ITESM Monterrey

Montalbán House

Client: Mr. and Mrs. Ricardo Montalbán
Size: 6,000 sq. ft.
Architectural Design: Ricardo Legorreta,
 Noé Castro
Design Team: Gerardo Alonso, Sydney
 Brisker
Architect of Record: Allen Sheriff
Structural Design: Kurily & Szymansky, Inc.
Mechanical Design: C. W. Eccleston
Interior Design and Landscape
 Architecture: Georgina Montalbán
Contractor: V. Stone Craft, Inc.

Pershing Square

Client: Pershing Square Property Owners
Size: 5 acres
Architectural Design: Ricardo Legorreta,
 Víctor Legorreta, Noé Castro
Design Team: Gerardo Alonso
Landscape Architecture: Hanna Olin Ltd.,
 Philadelphia/Laurie Olin
Executive Architect: Langdon Wilson
 Architecture Planning, Los Angeles
Coordination: Maguire Thomas Partners
Structural Design: Nabith Yussef &
 Associates
Artist: Barbara McCarren, Los Angeles
Contractor: Turner Construction

Rancho Santa Fe House

Client: Anonymous
Size: 16,000 sq. ft.
Architectural Design: Ricardo Legorreta,
 Noé Castro
Design Team: Gerardo Alonso, Emilio
 Guerrero, Sydney Brisker
Structural Design: Kurily Szymanski
 Tchirkow, Inc.
Mechanical Design: MBA/Mel Bilow
Electrical Design: Dalan Engineering
Interior Design: Bruce Gregga Interiors, Inc.
Landscape Architecture: Peter Walker/
 Martha Schwartz
Contractor: Weir Brothers, Inc.

Solana

Client: IBM Corporation, Maguire Thomas
 Partners
Client's Representative: Tom Allen
Size: 900 acres
Architectural Design: Ricardo Legorreta,
 Noé Castro
Design Team: Gerardo Alonso, Max
 Betancourt, Jorge Suárez
Master Plan Design Team: Legorreta
 Arquitectos, Peter Walker/Martha
 Schwartz, Barton Myers Associates,
 Mitchell Giurgola Architecture
Architect of Record: Harwood K. Smith &
 Partners, Leason Pomeroy Associates
Landscape Architecture: Peter
 Walker/Martha Schwartz
Design of IBM Westlake: Mitchell
 Giurgola Architecture

Greenberg House

Client: Mr. and Mrs. Arthur Greenberg
Size: 9,500 sq. ft.
Architectural Design: Ricardo Legorreta,
 Noé Castro
Design Team: Gerardo Alonso
Architect of Record: Sheriff & Associates
Structural Design: Kurily Szymanski
 Tchirkow
Mechanical Design: MB & A Mechanical
 Engineers
Electrical Design: G & W Consulting
 Electrical Engineers
Interior Design: James P. Sams, Inc.
Landscape Architecture: Lehrer &
 Sebastian
Contractor: L. B. Bovee & Sons
Awards: Architectural Record Award for
 excellence in planning and design

Plaza Reforma Office Building
Client: José Luis Rion/JORISA
Size: 215,000 sq. ft.
Architectural and Landscape Design:
    Ricardo Legorreta, Víctor Legorreta,
    Noé Castro
Design Team: Luis Esparza, Juan Carlos
    Nolasco
Structural Design: Heriberto Izquierdo
Electrical Design: Héctor Nieto
Contractor: Marberk Constructora, S. A.

House in Sonoma
Client: Anonymous
Size: 10,000 sq. ft.
Architectural Design: Ricardo Legorreta,
    Víctor Legorreta, Noé Castro
Design Team: Gerardo Alonso
Structural Design: Jack Lews Structural
    Design Engineers
Mechanical Design: G. M. Lim &
    Associates/George Lim
Contractor: Cello & Maudru Construction,
    Co./Bill Maudru

Monterrey Central Library
Client: Universidad Autónoma de Nuevo
    León
Size: 215,000 sq. ft.
Architectural and Interior Design: Ricardo
    Legorreta, Víctor Legorreta, Noé Castro
Design Team: Héctor Cavazos
Associate Architects: Armando Chávez,
    José Vigil
Structural Design: Alejandro Fierro, DYS,
    S. C.
Mechanical, Electrical, Plumbing Engineer:
    Tecno Proyectos, S. C.
Lighting Design: Starco Iluminación
Contractor: CB Consultores Asociados,
    S. A. de C. V./Guillermo Canales

Bankers Club
Client: Asociación de Banqueros de
    México
Size: 150,600 sq. ft.
Architectural and Interior Design: Ricardo
    Legorreta, Víctor Legorreta, Noé Castro
Design Team: Joaquin Pineda, Erica Krayer
Structural Design: Raúl Izquierdo
Mechanical Design: GHI
Electrical Design: Rimsa
Contractor: Gutsa

City of the Arts
Client: Consejo Nacional para la Cultura
    y las Artes
Size: 1,200,000 sq. ft.
Architectural Design: Ricardo Legorreta,
    Víctor Legorreta, Noé Castro
Design Team: Max Betancourt, Miguel
    Almaraz, Benjamín González, Francisco
    Vivas
Structural Design: DYS, S. C./Alejandro
    Fierro
Mechanical, Electrical, Plumbing Design:
    DIIN
HVAC: DYPRO
Acoustical Consultant: Jaffe, Holden,
    Scarbrough Acoustics, Inc.

Office Building in Monterrey
Client: Anonymous
Size: 130,000 sq. ft.
Architectural and Interior Design: Ricardo
    Legorreta, Víctor Legorreta, Noé Castro
Design Team: Héctor Cavazos, Miguel
    Almaraz
Structural Design: DYS, S. C./Alejandro
    Fierro
Mechanical, Electrical, Plumbing Design:
    Hecnie y Asociados, S. A./Héctor
    Nieto, Alejandro Borboa
Lighting Design: Fisher Marantz Reufro
    Stone
HVAC: Termo Control/Francisco
    Barrenechea
Contractor: Centro de Construcción/Lauro
    Chapa

San Antonio Main Library
Client: The City of San Antonio, Texas
Size: 240,000 sq. ft.
Architectural Design: Ricardo Legorreta,
    Víctor Legorreta, Noé Castro
Design Team: Miguel Almaraz, Gerardo
    Alonso, Benjamín González
Architect of Record: Johnson-Dempsey &
    Associates
Associate Architect: Davis Sprinkle &
    Robey Architects
Project Management: 3D International
Interior Design: Ford, Powell & Carson/
    Humberto Saldaña/Callins & Associates
Structural Design: Danish-Lundy Pinnell
Mechanical, Electrical, Plumbing Engineer:
    Goetting & Associates
Landscape Design: James Cooper
Artists: Stephen Antanakos (neon light),
    Jesse Treviño (mural)
Contractor: H. A. Lott, Inc.

La Colorada House
Client: Anonymous
Site: 4.9 acres
Floor Area: 10,225 sq. ft.
Architectural Design: Ricardo Legorreta,
    Víctor Legorreta, Noé Castro
Associate Architects: Armando Chávez,
    José Vigil
Landscape Design: Eliseo Arredondo
Structural Design: Ricardo Camacho
Mechanical Design: Hubard Instalaciones,
    S. A. de C. V.
Contractor: Miguel Campero

Casa Jacinta and Víctor
Client: Mr. & Mrs. Víctor Legorreta
Size: 4,008 sq. ft.
Architectural Design, Interior and
    Landscape Architecture: Víctor Legorreta
Structural Design: Ricardo Camacho
Mechanical Design: Hecnie y Asociados,
    S. A./Héctor Nieto, Alejandro Borboa
Contractor: Pedro Samano

Akle House
Client: José and Magda Akle
Size: 2,700 sq. ft.
Architectural Design, Interior and
    Landscape Architecture: Ricardo
    Legorreta, Víctor Legorreta, Noé Castro
Design Team: Pablo Rivera
Structural Design: Humberto Panuco
Mechanical Design: Alejandro Borboa
Contractor: Efren Emeterio

Metropolitan Cathedral
Client: Archdiocese of Managua
Sponsor: Tom Monaghan
Size: 28,000 sq. ft.
Architectural and Interior Design: Ricardo
    Legorreta, Víctor Legorreta, Noé Castro
Design Team: Francisco Vivas, Guillermo
    Díaz de Sandi, Miguel Almaraz
Project Management: NATEX, Co./José
    Terán
Structural Design: Walker P. Moore
Mechanical Design: Lamsa Ingenieros, Co.
Electrical Design: Enrique Hernández
Lighting Design: Fisher Marantz Reufro
    Stone